SEDUCTIVE SELLING

WARNING

This book contains explicit material
which could benefit your competitors

SEDUCTIVE SELLING

THE ULTIMATE GUIDE TO WOOING
A CUSTOMER

Kit Sadgrove

KOGAN
PAGE

To Alexandra: most seductive of women

First published in 1994

Kogan Page Limited
120 Pentonville Road
London N1 9JN

British Library Cataloguing in Publication Data

A CIP record for this book is available from the British Library.

ISBN 0 7494 1214 3 (PB)   0 7494 1361 1 (HB)

Typeset by DP Photosetting, Aylesbury, Bucks
Printed in England by Clays Ltd, St Ives plc

Contents

Preface   7

About the Author   8

Introduction

  1.   Sex and selling   11

Consider what relationship you want

  2.   Who are you after?   23

  3.   The customer: the object of your passion   30

  4.   Your competitors   38

Create the relationship

  5.   Make the buyer warm to you   45

  6.   Getting through   54

  7.   Seductive writing   59

Communicate fully

  8.   The seduction process   69

  9.   Building a relationship   85

10.   Use your body   96

11. Seductive words   105

12. Overcoming resistance   120

Climax

13. Closing in   137

Continue the relationship

14. Keeping it up   149

15. Seductive service   160

Summary

16. The facts of life   175

Preface

In this book, the buyer has been treated as male, purely for the sake of brevity and consistency. The buyer could equally be female, and often is.

Both men and women have seductive skills. So *Seductive Selling* is aimed at all sales people, whether male or female, because the lessons simply apply to us all.

Seductive Selling is also available as an in-house training course. If you would like more information, write to Kit Sadgrove, Honeycombe House, Bagley, Wedmore BS28 4TD. Tel: (0934) 713572.

About the author

Kit Sadgrove is a principal consultant with an international management consultancy.

He has worked for companies such as ICI, Mars, Weetabix, British Rail, Barratt Homes, the National Health Service and National Power.

Kit has sold advertising, beer, circular stairs, computer networks, confectionery, eggs, floor covering, fitted kitchens, insurance, telephones, soap, tinned vegetables, toilet cubicles, toys and washing up liquid.

He is the author of *The Green Manager's Handbook*, and *Writing to Sell*. He lives in Somerset with his wife and five children.

Introduction

Sex and Selling

Sex and selling are similar activities. Both are a quest.

You have to find the right person, understand their needs and woo them. Then you consummate the relationship. Later, you try to maintain it.

And that's the subject of *Seductive Selling*: to show the best ways of finding, winning and keeping a customer.

The principles are simple. You should treat your customer like you treat your lover. Win the customer's respect. Keep the customer happy. Keep offering more than the competition. Never take the customer for granted.

Seductive Selling traces the course of a relationship. Each chapter looks at a specific aspect of seduction. What words do you use? How can you look your best? The same issues are found in love and selling. Competitors in love are like competitors in selling. A proposal of marriage is like a sales proposal.

The principles of *Seductive Selling* apply to all markets. So whether you sell power stations or biscuits, the book offers you valuable insights on better selling.

As Table 1 shows, the way you tackle a lover is similar to the way you handle a buyer.

Seductive Selling applies anywhere you need to woo, win and keep a customer. It applies especially to the more complex types of selling, such as:

- Key account or national account selling;
- Selling professional services, such as accountancy, the law, architecture, or advertising;

How the lover and the buyer relate

Love	Selling
The lover	The buyer
Other suitors	The competition
Asking for a date	Appointment setting
The date	The sales interview
Chat up line	The sales pitch
Sexually diseased partner	Financially unsound customer
Taking precautions, practising safe sex	Taking precautions through credit checks or setting credit limits
Becoming infected	Bad debt
Body language	Body language
Telephone style	Telephone style
Love letter	Tender or quotation
A proposal	A proposal
Improving your chances	Avoiding the cold sell
Equality in love	Teamwork in selling
Overcoming reluctance	Overcoming objections
The consummation	The sale
A one-night stand	A one-off sale
Strip show	Presentation
Making a pass	Asking for the order
Maintaining the relationship	Customer satisfaction
Attentiveness	Service
Flattery, charm, encouragement	Advertising
Faithfulness, monogamy	Integrity

Table 1 **Love is similar to selling in many ways**

- Tendering, such as in construction and engineering;
- Long-term project-based work, such as aerospace or defence;
- Industrial selling;
- Developing formal links with a customer (where, for example, you become an approved or preferred supplier. This is increasingly happening as a result of BS 5750 (ISO 9000) and the influence of Japanese business methods).

The book emphasises the benefits of honesty, caring, and long-term relationships. These values are relevant to both lovers and customers.

Seductive Selling will help you assess whether your selling technique is as effective as it could be. It will help you to be more effective, perhaps even gain promotion. You might want to run it as a topic in a sales meeting.

It is also a good idea to have a fresh look at *Seductive Selling* every six months. You'll find different chapters hold new interest as time goes by.

WHAT YOU'LL GET FROM *SEDUCTIVE SELLING*

Maybe you reckon you're a good lover? After all, you've been chatting up the other sex since you were a teenager.

Selling often attracts good lovers: people who are smart, confident, and at ease with other people.

But selling is more than just good conversation and a relaxed manner. And being a good lover takes more than wearing attractive clothes and being sensuous.

The people who get to the top are the ones who never stop learning. They recognise that they can always improve. They can take other people's suggestions and adapt them to suit their own needs.

And just because you've done something for a long time, it doesn't mean to say you're doing it well. A little while ago, I was talking about a sales person. I said, 'He's very experienced: he's been doing this job for ten years.' My colleague replied, 'No, he's been doing the job the same way, every year, for ten years. That means he has only one year's experience, repeated ten times.'

So now is the time to look at how you should approach your lover and your customers. This book could tell you a lot – about yourself, your lover and your customers.

You may never again see things the same way. For like love, *Seductive Selling* is a true voyage of discovery.

THE WORLD HAS CHANGED – AND SELLING HAS TO CHANGE TOO

'Customer service' is a buzz word in many companies. It is especially popular in the once nationalised industries in both the West and the former communist countries.

Much of this attention on customer service has concentrated on the service provided by operating staff – railway guards, gas showroom staff and government benefits employees. Less attention has been paid to the changing needs of the buyer in thousands of organisations across the world.

But the Japanese have changed the way buyers work. Today customers seek co-operation not conflict; they want long-term customer-supplier relationships, not one-off sales. Buyers now have a different attitude towards the sales people they meet. That means you have to change, too.

Today, the buyer wants a deeper, closer relationship with his suppliers. The Technical Services Manager of Woolworth says, 'We say to our suppliers: "This is how we see our business with you for the next three years. Now you tell us what you're going to do for us."' This is very different from the old picture of a salesman who says '100g coffee is cheap this week; how many do you want?'

Traditionally, sales people have been taught to concentrate on just the immediate sales interview. They were taught to get Attention, Interest, Desire and Agreement (known as AIDA). But as *Seductive Selling* shows, you now have to look at a much wider period of time. In particular, you should be concerned about the period following delivery of the order.

You also have to adopt a different attitude towards the buyer. It is imperative to develop a long-term relationship with your buyer, to get close to him, and to develop a culture

The two main differences between seductive selling and old selling		
	Old style selling	Seductive selling
Duration of relationship	Brief	Long term
Style of relationship	Conflict	Sharing, mutual advantage

Table 2 **Durable and harmonious relationships result from using the** Seductive Selling **method**

of sharing. In other words, you need to treat your buyer like a lover, and adopt the methods of *Seductive Selling*. This is summarised in Table 2.

THE ADVANTAGES OF USING THE *SEDUCTIVE SELLING* METHOD

Seductive Selling gives you an advantage over your competitors, because it adopts a different method of selling. Treating your customer like a lover will give you the benefits shown in Table 3.

HOW TO BECOME A SEDUCTIVE SELLER

Whether you're seeking a lover or a customer, the process is the same. Both love and selling processes have five phases. These are the **Five Cs of Seductive Selling**. They are: **Consider, Create, Communicate, Climax and Continue.**

Consider

Consider what sort of person would be most likely to want you.

The advantages of the seductive selling method	
The old way	**Using the seductive selling approach**
The buyer responds to you defensively.	The buyer welcomes you as a friend.
You are under pressure to 'sell, sell, sell'.	You face less stress. You expect the buyer to buy only what he needs.
You adopt techniques designed to trick or force the buyer into a sale.	You avoid techniques which might be seen as dishonest and which could cause the buyer to mistrust you.
You conceal weaknesses about your product.	You openly express reservations where a product may not be suitable.
You seek short-term business, at the expense of repeat orders.	You seek long-term business, at the expense of short-term orders.
You seek an ever widening number of buyers, sometimes at ever increasing distances.	You develop a core of loyal buyers.

Table 3 **Which style of selling would you prefer to adopt?**

In love, would that person be:

- tall or short?
- fond of rock music or opera?
- located in the city or the country?

In selling:

- What sort of title would he have?
- What sort of industry would he work for?
- Would his company be large or small?

In this part we also analyse the competitors who are vying for your customer.

Create

You have to create the relationship. In love this means finding a prospective lover, and inviting them out. In selling, it means fixing an appointment or sending direct mail.

This is a crucial phase, because it is the starting point of a process which ultimately leads to the Climax. Until you have picked up the phone or sent a letter, no sales can take place.

In this part we see how you can get your prospective lover or customer to warm towards you. Avoiding a cold call is crucial, because it won't produce success. We look at appointment setting (which lovers call 'asking for a date'). And we examine the way you communicate in writing. The right sort of letter, to either a customer or to a lover, can lead you towards the sale or the consummation.

Communicate

This is the core of the process, which takes place at the sales interview. This stage requires all your communication skills.

Communicating means listening as well as talking. It means expressing with your eyes and your body movements. It means understanding the other person's needs, and achieving a dialogue.

There are four chapters in this part. They deal with the seduction process, body language, the words you use, and overcoming resistance.

Climax

This is the moment you have been waiting for. The buyer gives you an order, or the lover asks you to make love. It makes the uncertainty and the long wait worthwhile.

Only when the other person trusts you and needs you will the climax take place. So it is essential to understand what is going on in the other person's mind. Here we examine how you close in on a buyer or a lover.

Continue

You have to work at this relationship if you want it to continue. Excellent customer service will keep your buyer satisfied, while constant attention will maintain your lover's affection.

In this part, we consider why customer service has become more important, and how you can categorise your customers. Then we look at ways you can improve the quality of your service.

Finally, we come to a chapter called **The facts of life**. It reviews all the lessons of *Seductive Selling*.

The route to seductive selling, whether to a lover or a customer is shown in Table 4. The last column of this Table (headed 'Chapter') shows where to find each phase in the book: you don't need to read the book from start to finish if you don't want to. You may find it helpful to look at a specific issue, like Chapter 11 on Seductive Words.

You may not be involved in the entire process. Some customers are self-selecting; they present themselves at a department store or car showroom. But the basic task of selling your product to the customer (Chapters 8 to 15) holds true for every sales person.

In the next chapter we start at the beginning of the *Seductive Selling* process. We begin by looking at the sort of person you have in mind as a lover or a customer.

The route to seductive selling

The Five Cs	How to find a lover	How to find a customer	Chapter
1. *Consider*	Identify the type of person likely to want you as a lover	Identify the type of customer likely to buy from you	2. Who are you after? 3. The customer 4. Your competitors
2. *Create*	Locate a potential lover	Locate a potential customer	5. Make the buyer warm to you
	Seek agreement for a date	Get agreement for a meeting	6. Getting through 7. Seductive Writing
3. *Communicate*	Go on the date	Meet the customer	8. The seduction process
	Understand the lover's needs	Assess the buyer's needs	9. Building a relationship
	Present yourself in the best light	Compile and present a package which meets those needs	10. Use your body 11. Seductive words
	Overcome resistance	Overcome objection	12. Overcoming resistance
4. *Climax*	Make love	Close the sale	13. Closing in
5. *Continue*	Maintain the relationship	Maintain the relationship in order to obtain future sales	14. Keeping it up 15. Seductive service

Table 4 **The process of finding a lover and a customer is the same**

Consider what relationship you want

Who are you After?

Whether you want a lover or a customer, you have to start by asking yourself the two essential questions shown in Table 5.

Many people *think* they know the answers, but fewer have thought about the questions properly. There are many things you need to know about your potential customer; and this information will help you to win a sale.

YOU DON'T HAVE TO CHASE THEM ALL

You don't need to chase every potential lover. You know from experience that you'll have more success with some types of people than with others. Whether you go for barmaids, coal miners, or PhD students is up to you. But what you are doing is segmenting your market.

What about your product? Do you hope to cover the whole

Finding a lover	Finding a customer
1. What sort of a person would want me as a lover?	1. Who wants to buy my product?
2. Where will I find that person?	2. Where will I find that person?

Table 5 **Two fundamental questions to ask**

market? If so, you risk pleasing no one. The most obvious segments in most markets are price (many markets have two, three or even more price brackets). The market can also be segmented by the customer's age (think about house purchase, holidays or clothing). Gender and geographical location are two other common ones. Table 6 helps you decide which segments to target, both in love and in selling.

Targeting your effort	
Segments in selling	**Segments in love**
Size (for example, less than £m turnover, or over £250m)	Gender
Location (for example, South West France)	Age
Industry (Plastics)	Attractiveness
Job title (Chief Engineer)	Politics
Timing (spring or summer purchasing)	Interests
Attitude to price, quality, delivery and other variables	Introvert/extrovert
Application of the product (for example, carpets can be used in commercial premises, a domestic hall or in the bedroom)	Intelligence/education
Role in the chain (OEM, wholesaler, consumer)	Aspirations
External requirements to buy (for example, new legislation)	Social class

Table 6 **Focusing on likely candidates helps you concentrate your efforts, understand the specific needs, and compare success rates between segments.**

WHERE DO YOU FIND YOUR LOVER?

If you're looking for a lover you probably go where crowds gather – pubs, discos and nightclubs; places where you meet lots of others who are young and single. Numbers are important: the more people in the room, the higher your chances of finding someone to love.

It doesn't always work well. An event that is so noisy that you can't talk isn't necessarily the best place. Some people visit art galleries to meet potential lovers.

Chess clubs, photography societies and pressure groups often flourish because they enable people with similar interests to meet up. They let you talk 'legitimately' to people of the opposite sex. It is wise to choose a club preferred by members of the opposite sex. A ballet school may not be the best place to find a male, and a civil engineering association may have few women!

There are lessons here for selling. The obvious outlets are not the only places to find a customer. In fact, novel ways of finding a customer are often more successful. For example, in the UK some firms have been very successful in selling housewares not through the usual department stores but by mail order or by door-to-door selling.

PLAYING THE NUMBERS' GAME

Table 7 shows the effort required to win an order. In this market the sales person has to write tenders to win orders. Only one in three of his tenders are successful.

To get a tender, he has to visit the customer to examine their needs. But only one in three potential customers ask for a tender, so he has to make nine sales visits. To set appointments for those nine visits, the company has to keep generating sales leads. They can come from advertisements, from telesales or direct mail. They can also come from unexpected sources, and some examples are shown in Table 7.

Your own 'numbers game' may have different figures. It may have a different shaped pyramid. But the principle remains true:

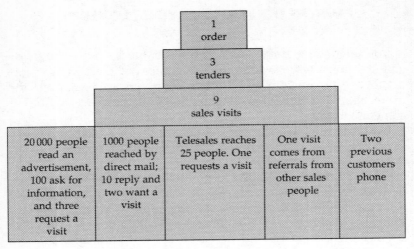

Table 7 **What are the numbers in your business?**

the more people you contact, the more sales you win. You also need to know your success ratio, shown above as 1:3:9. You can work out your own numbers by answering the questions in Table 8.

The same process applies if you are managing a set of accounts. Only a proportion of your accounts will buy in any one month. To reach your target, you will have to visit enough accounts.

Timing is crucial, too. How long does it take you to win a sale? You have to convert a 'suspect' (someone who might buy your product) into a 'prospect' (someone who is thinking of buying your product). Then you have to convert the prospect into a firm order. In a few markets, this process is instant, but in many it takes weeks, months or even years. So if today you stop promoting your business, you'll have fewer visits booked next month. And in six months' time, you'll have fewer orders.

One of my colleagues moved into a new territory. It took him nine months of prospecting before he won a single order. Now he says, 'The actions I take today will have no effect on our sales for nearly a year'.

Working out the numbers game for yourself	
The questions to ask	**The answers**
How much business do you need to keep the business in profit?	
What is value of the average order?	
How many average-sized orders do you need?	
How many tenders must you write to win a sale?	
How many visits must you make to win a tender?	

Table 8   **Can you put the numbers in the box provided?**

THE CUSTOMERS WHO OFFER THEMSELVES TO YOU

Later in the book (Chapter 14) we consider the different types of customers and the way they behave. But it is worth noting here that there are two types of customers whom you don't have to go and woo – the customers who ask to place an order without being asked. These are either **Former Lovers** or **Suitors**.

Former lovers: Former lovers are customers who have bought from you in the past. It pays to stay friends with your Former Lovers by keeping in touch with them. Nothing beats the sensation of hearing from a Former Lover who rings up and says, 'I may have another job for you.'

Suitors: A Suitor is someone who has not bought from your company before, but wants to buy. The Suitor rings up and asks about buying your product. Most companies wonder where the Suitor heard of them, and why he has decided to ring them up. Far fewer ask the question, 'Where did you hear of us?'

The Suitor is like a pop fan who has seen his idol on television and has fallen in love. The reality of the pop idol often falls short of the carefully presented image. Often the idol is weak, a drunk, or incapable of giving love. Does your Suitor face the same disappointment?

Sometimes customer service falls short of the carefully honed advertisement. You need a system for handling Suitors. Other people in your firm may not have your 'people' skills: it's worth seeing how a Suitor gets treated. It's also worth checking to see what happens to Suitors who write a fan letter. This is when the Suitor asks for a brochure. Many companies fail to send the information. Still more fail to follow up the enquiry.

THE NUMBERS GAME IN LOVE

Imagine you're looking for a lover. You live in a village of 100 people. You can sit down and work through the numbers.

Of the 100 villagers, only 50 are female. Of these, only 10 are aged 18-30 and unmarried. Of the 10, five are ugly, three are stupid and one is boring. That leaves only one girl, and she has her eye on a young farmer.

So to find your lover you have to look farther afield. In fact, some social scientists have calculated that you need a city of two million people to find a lover who suits your needs. Two million fellow inhabitants, 100 acquaintances, 10 good friends, one lover. It's called 'the numbers game'.

STAYING CLEAN

You wouldn't want to make love with someone who had a sexually transmitted disease, let alone Aids. But you can't tell who is carrying disease; and that means you should always take precautions, by practising safe sex.

It's the same in selling. You want to avoid customers who are unsound. You can take precautions by doing credit checks; and if you're in any doubt you should not take the risk. If you decide to accept a new customer, there are ways to prevent yourself from becoming infected. For example, you can ask for payment in advance or stage payments. Or you can set credit limits.

In love, a sexually diseased partner can infect you. And a

financially unstable customer can weaken your business through bad debt. This means lovers, like customers, carry risks. You know the dangers: so it's up to you to take precautions.

ACTION POINTS

♥ Ask yourself what sort of person needs your products, and where you will find them.

♥ Segment the market to achieve greater success.

♥ Play the numbers game by contacting enough prospects to achieve enough sales.

♥ Keep in touch with former customers.

♥ Take precautions: avoid dealing with financially unsound customers.

3

The Customer: The Object of Your Passion

In the old days, you knew where you stood. The man made the advances, while the woman responded. The man earned the money, the woman stayed at home. The man went down the pub, the woman brought up the children.

All that has changed. There has been a revolution in both sex and selling. Women expect a more equal share in life. They are equal partners with men. In business, they make expert sales people. In sex, they expect an orgasm.

The days of the one-night stand are over, too. Your lover now wants a long-term relationship.

THE CHANGES IN LOVE

Women are now more likely to take the initiative in love. They are more likely to ask for a date, or initiate love making. But they also feel frustrated by men who are not emotionally involved, and who can't express their feelings. They are less willing to put up with poor quality relationships: more divorces are filed by women than men.

Men are less confident than they were in the past. They think that their sexual advances could be interpreted as sexual harassment. They feel threatened by successful women who are not financially reliant on a man. They don't understand what

women want, and they are confused by the sometimes contradictory messages they receive.

This means that men and women have to work harder at their
relationships.

Women have to help men understand the new rules of love.
They have to show them that a relationship will be successful if it
is built on mutual understanding and respect.

Men have to curb their traditional predatory instincts. They
need to recognise that women need to be wooed and cared for.
They need to take a greater share of life's chores, including
childcare and household work. And they need to accept women's
individuality and ambitions.

THE CHANGES IN SELLING

There have been many similar changes in selling. The customer
also wants a long-term relationship, in the business sense. No
longer can a sales person expect to walk in to a customer and
collect an order automatically.

Table 9 shows some of the changes that have taken place, and
suggests ways of adapting to those changes.

WHO IS YOUR CUSTOMER?

Often will you be dealing with more than one buyer, as a number
of people in the organisation may pay a part in the decision. This
is called a **Decision Making Unit**, or **DMU**. Find out who
comprises the DMU, and ensure that all its members are willing
to buy your product. Table 10 shows the different people who
may be involved in the purchase.

WHY DO PEOPLE BUY?

Customers have a range of needs, and their motives can be
different from the product benefits you are selling. In particular,
they buy to get the following personal advantages:

Twelve changes in the market

Changes among customers	The way to respond
1. Most markets have fewer buying points, as the multiples take over more of the distribution chain.	Put greater emphasis on key account selling and trade marketing. Give better service to national account customers.
2. There is often more than one person doing the buying. Engineering, marketing, IT or human resources managers may also be involved. Today's buyer expects you to be part of his team.	Find out who else is involved. Understand their needs and seek their views. Become more involved in the customer's business. Provide a tailor-made solution to the customer's problem.
3. Customers are concerned about quality in their organisation and among their suppliers. Customers have learnt from the Japanese that the supplier is an essential part of the quality programme.	Improve the quality of your work. The quality of the sales team (that is to say, *you*) will distinguish one supplier from another. Your ability to give the customer a better solution to his problem will be a key factor in your success.
4. Customers want longer-term relationships with fewer suppliers who are more involved.	Develop a long-term relationship with the customer.
5. Customers are making greater use of computers.	Use computers more thoroughly and just as effectively. They will give you better information, and help provide more effective answers to customers' concerns. Consider linking into the customer's computer system.

Table 9   **Changes in the market, and how to respond to them**

Twelve changes in the market (cont.)

6. Improved customer service has become required.	Be ready to respond to customer's queries and complaints.
7. There are faster changes in retail stocking.	Be able to offer new products.
8. There is faster innovation in new products.	Preempt the competitors who are always ready to take your place.
9. There is more awareness of concepts like segmentation and brand identity.	Treat customers as individuals.
10. Consumers are more sophisticated.	Upgrade the quality and modernity of your products.
11. Many of today's purchases are more complex. The product may now be a package which includes training, installation or merchandising. It might involve co-operative advertising or complex volume-related payments. It might require dealer support or a telephone hotline.	Involve the rest of your company. A sales person now needs to be an account manager. You have to liaise with the rest of your organisation. Use your colleagues' different skills to provide the best product or service.
12. There are more laws and self-regulation governing business (for example, in selling financial services).	Maintain a high level of integrity in product formula, selling and publicity.

Types of purchaser			
Role	**Characteristics**	**How to sell**	**Your own situation**
Initial contact	Not always the person with the power to buy. It could be a secretary or a clerical person.	Find out who he reports to, and whether he has authority to buy.	
Decision maker	The person with the power to authorise the go-ahead.	You may need to meet this person, perhaps on a second visit. His needs may be different from those of the initial contact.	
User	The person who will use the equipment or service.	Find out what the user's real needs are. This could give you an advantage over the competition, because you will be seen to understand the user better.	
Buyer	Often has a formal buying department role. Watch out for obstructive behaviour, which can result from frustration or hostility at a perceived attack on his power.	Work with him to agree the specification. Check for any pre-contract requirements, such as ISO 9000.	
Financier	May be the Financial Director. Will be concerned to keep costs down.	Emphasise value for money, reliability and track record.	
Influencer	He could have a positive or negative influence. He could be a user in a sister company who has experience of your product. Or he could be a Board member in the same company.	Establish from the decision maker the names of those who might influence the decision. Involve them at the earliest opportunity. Make sure they have all relevant information.	

Table 10   **Many people may be involved in making the decision to buy**

- Wealth, a bargain, savings, to save money
- Self esteem
- Improved appearance, better looks
- A simpler life
- Knowledge, new skills
- Popularity
- Security, self preservation
- Save time or effort
- Status, power
- Pleasure

These are very simple and basic needs. They apply whether your customer is buying software development, a surgical operation, or a packet of tea bags. On the surface, they seem to be buying a product that you are selling. But in reality, they are looking to satisfy a deeper psychological need.

Buyers also make compromises. They buy a product which satisfies more of their needs. So they may buy your product even if it isn't the most advanced or the newest. A recent survey showed that people preferred one supermarket because it scored well (but not top) on most of the issues which were important to them – such as low prices, convenient location, friendly staff and car parking. Other supermarkets had lower prices or better car parks, but none scored as consistently on all the topics.

Sometimes we have preconceptions about a buyer's needs, and those preconceptions can be wrong. The buyer's real needs can turn out to be quite different. Take the case of a fast food restaurant, as shown in Table 11.

PEOPLE BUY IMAGE

People also buy perceptions. They want to buy from a particular company because it has a certain image. They are buying a package of emotions. There is no real reason why one person buys a Ford, another buys a Nissan, and a third buys a Renault. Each is buying something which reflects himself, or something he aspires to be. A survey showed that US computer firms were buying Japanese chips because they *perceived* them to be of better quality than American ones.

I worked for a financial services company which offered investors poor value for money – yet hundreds of thousands of people invest with this company. It has an image which they like,

Customer wants and expectations	
The restaurant's view	**The customers' view**
Existing The restaurant thinks its customers buy because it is: – Cheap – Clean – Friendly – Stylish	Customers really buy because the restaurant is: – Conveniently located – Clean – Safe
Future The restaurant thinks its customers would like: – More speed – New menus	The customers would really like: – Bigger portions – More comfortable seating – Longer opening hours

Table 11 **The needs of a fast food customer may be different from what the restaurant imagines**

and it has sales people they like. In part, the customer is buying the image which you convey. And if you don't convey the image he is seeking, he won't buy your product.

You should consider whether your customer sees you as friendly or businesslike, traditional or innovative, thoughtful or dynamic.

BE SUPPORTIVE

Think of yourself as the customer's assistant. Look at the problem from his point of view. Offer him the advice that his assistant would offer.

Imagine you sell haulage. As his 'assistant' you say to the customer, 'You need a supplier who is utterly reliable. You don't want to spend time worrying about haulage. You want the supplier to know the business, and to have experience in the industry. There are some cheap firms around, but their drivers aren't going to present the right image to customers.'

This is a more effective sales pitch than saying, 'We have a modern fleet of 42 lorries, of all sizes, capable of transporting all types of goods'.

By looking at the problem from the assistant's point of view, you begin to appreciate what the customer really wants. It makes you look dispassionate, and interested in the customer's needs. It also shows you understand the customer's business.

Position yourself as a member of the customer's team. Turn your buyer-seller relationship into a joint venture. Identify what will make your customer successful, and help him achieve that – providing that you, too, share in the reward by winning his business.

ACTION POINTS

♥ Respond to the changes in buying by developing a long-term relationship with the customer.

♥ Become more involved in customer's business. Provide tailor-made solutions.

♥ Involve the other departments of your organisation in providing superior customer service.

♥ Remember that the buyer does not work alone. Work out how different people in the customer's company will affect the sale.

♥ Understand the real reasons why your customers buy. Emphasise these reasons to the customer.

♥ Be supportive to the customer. Imagine yourself as his assistant.

Your Competitors

If you're competing for a lover's attentions, you need to understand the strengths and weaknesses of the other suitors. Start by *understanding* the competition. What attracts your potential lover to them? What do they give her that you don't?

The same applies in selling. What do your competitors give your customer that you don't? Do they visit more often? Or do they entertain better?

WHAT YOU NEED TO KNOW

Table 12 contains some of the questions you should be asking. This will tell you how to respond to competitive pressures in the market place. It will tell you what products to promote and how to counter customers' objections.

You can go a stage further by checking the quality of each of your competitors on specific topics. This is often called **benchmarking**, and an example is shown in Table 13. Find out the answers by asking your customers. Give marks on a scale of one to five, with five for excellence.

MAKING IMPROVEMENTS

The grid in Table 13 will help you analyse the areas where you need to improve. You may need to involve other departments to

Information about a competitor
What is the image of the competitor?
How loyal are its customers?
What does it do well? What can you do to match it?
What are its weaknesses? Which weaknesses are important to customers?
How do the competitors' products compare with yours?
How does their level of service compare with yours?
What costs do the competitors have? This will help you decide whether to respond to demands for discounts, or how to price an estimate.

Table 12 **What you need to know about your competitors**

create change. As a sales person, you are closest to the customer, and therefore it is your responsibility to insist on improvements.

Sales people are sometimes accused of only asking for bigger discounts to sell the products. It is a natural urge when you are facing price competition. But your company is in real danger when your competitors start to meet customers' needs better than you can. When that happens, it is up to you to make your organisation aware of the threat.

DEALING WITH COMPETITORS

When, as a lover, you analyse the suitors who are competing against you, there are only four strategies you can adopt. You can:

1. ignore the competitors;
2. knock the competitors;
3. give up, and look for another lover; or
4. out-perform the competition, and win.

	Your company	Your competitors		
		A	B	C
Product				
Product quality				
Product design or functions				
Price				
Speed of delivery				
Availability				
Customer service				
Frequency of sales visits or communication				
Attitude of sales staff				
Extent of customer entertainment				
Attitude of customer service staff				
Promotion				
Advertising and sales promotion				
Effectiveness of sales literature				
Total				

Assess your competitors

Table 13 **Benchmarking in selling. You will need to amend this table to suit your market. Some categories may not apply; others may need to be added**

Companies have the same problem. There's often a bigger firm around, and lots of smaller competitors. All are vying for the same customers, and all of them have different strengths and weaknesses. Like lovers, firms have the same four options.

- **Ignoring the competitors** happens if you think you're invincible. The car industry ignored the threat of Nissan and Toyota for a long time, thinking it had nothing to learn from them. Almost too late it started to look at what was attracting the customer to Japanese cars.

  Other people ignore the competitors out of ignorance or lack of interest. This is an equally dangerous strategy. Your competitors loom large in your customers' minds – they are constantly knocking on their doors.

- **Knocking the competition** depends on your position in the market. If you're the market leader and you criticise the smaller firms, customers will think you're worried about the competition. Your comments will also give the competition free publicity. So it's rarely a good idea for a market leader to talk about its competitors.

  If you're a newcomer to the market, or you have a small market share, you haven't got much to lose. Likewise, if you have a strong competitive advantage, you stand to gain. So knocking the competition is appropriate only if the conditions are right. You should only do it when the buyer has said he buys from them, or intends to do so.

  Never make a *general* criticism about the competition, such as 'I wouldn't buy from them'. Always make a specific point, such as 'We're 20% cheaper', or 'They only have 8 colours, whereas we have 15'.

  Knocking the competition should always be preceded by praising them, as in 'They're an excellent firm. But...'

- **Giving up** is easy. Lots of companies do this. They neglect their core business. They start buying companies, or set up new businesses unconnected with what they currently do. The danger is that the competitors will start to undermine their core business even further. You, personally, could give up by going to work in another industry or even another career, but you will always find competitors wherever you go. The fact that you are reading this book shows that you are looking not to quit but to win; and that brings us to the next strategy.

- **Outperforming the competition**. If you agree that knocking the competition and giving up are not ideal solutions, you're left with the fourth option, that of outperforming the competitors. That means your company has to improve in all areas. One of the most important areas is customer service, of treating your customer like a lover. You have to be more seductive, and show that you care. And that is the subject of the rest of this book.

ACTION POINTS

♥ Set out to understand how you compare against the competitors.

♥ Use the information to adapt your response to customers' demands and requirements.

♥ Decide how you can overcome competitors' strengths, and make use of their weaknesses.

♥ Decide in advance your policy on knocking the competition. Be careful how you use it.

Create the Relationship

Make the Buyer Warm to You

Cold calls are the least likely way to get a sale. You wouldn't stroll into a pub, walk up to someone and say 'Fancy some sex?'

To achieve success in love, as we saw in Chapter 2, you need to identify places where you will find the right kind of person. Then you need to give your intended lover time to know you, trust you and want you.

Yet too many companies expect sales people to meet an unknown prospect and come out with a sale.

COLD CALLING DOESN'T SELL A PRODUCT

A customer won't buy on a cold call. But cold calling is common in many companies. An insurance salesman is still expected to do telephone canvassing, which means phoning people whose names are obtained from the telephone book.

People only buy when they are in the mood. The insurance salesman may strike lucky – he may find someone who is thinking about buying insurance. But the other 99 per cent of people he contacts will reject him. There has to be a better way.

SHORTLISTING THE CANDIDATES

The first task is to identify the 'suspects', ie the people who might buy. For our insurance salesman, these are house buyers, couples who have just had a baby, or someone who has just started work. In short, they are people who are going through a lifestyle change, and are looking to alter the balance of income and expenditure. In other words, you have to know something about potential customers before you approach them.

In Table 14 we look at ways of ensuring that the buyer actually welcomes you into his office. You do this by only visiting prospects with whom you have an established link.

Establishing a link

Establishing a link with a prospect is a good way of avoiding a cold call. Here are some links you can use.

- Do you personally know the customer? Have you sold to him before?
- If it is a business call, do you know someone else in the company who could refer you to the buyer?
- Has your business sold to the company before? If you keep computerised customer records, treat them as the valuable tools they are.
- Have you a contact outside your company who could refer you to the prospect?
- Has the company received any publicity in the media? This will allow to ring up and say, 'I read that you're developing a new product. You might find our packaging system could match its high-tech image.'
- Can you meet someone through a mutual friend?
- Can you meet someone at a social event?

I once rang a manufacturer of customised briefcases, looking to buy a set of sample cases for the sales force. To my surprise the salesman showed me a link. He showed me that my company had bought similar products from his firm a few years previously. It was no coincidence that he won the order.

Table 14 **Establishing a link means that the prospect will be well-disposed towards you**

LEADING UP TO THE BIG EVENT

You have to get your intended lover in the mood for love. Maybe you take him or her to dinner; go out dancing; go back to your house. Your lover may now want to make love.

It's the same with customers. If you can put the customer in the mood to buy, if you lay out your stall correctly, the chances are he'll buy. Table 15 indicates the strategies most likely to achieve success.

THE INDIRECT APPROACH

There are two ways to get a date. You can ring someone up, and say, 'Would you like a date?' or you can use a more sophisticated method. Find out what your would-be lover enjoys, then find an appropriate event and mention it. You could say, 'I hear there's a rock festival next Saturday'. If your lover shows a buying signal by saying, 'How wonderful', you can say, 'Why don't we go to it?'

This indirect or *oblique* approach also applies to selling. You find out what the buyer needs, and offer him help – without making an overt sales pitch. Fitted kitchen companies do it by offering a free design service. Table 16 contains some more ideas on the oblique approach.

You can also ask for advice or help. I sometimes send out questionnaires. The responses tell me a lot about the needs of different companies, and when I send them a report on the findings of the survey, it gives me an opportunity to ring up and discuss it with them.

Remember – the buyer is simply someone who wants to solve a problem. Unless he has the title of Purchasing Manager, he won't see himself as a buyer – that is just the way you see him. Your job is to help him solve his problems.

THE GOOD LOVER-GOOD SELLER QUIZ

How good are you – as a lover and as a seller? This quiz sets out to discover the answers.

Is your customer ready to buy?		
Customers are less likely to buy when:	Customers are more likely to buy when:	The strategy to adopt
They are sought out by the sales person	They seek out the sales person	Seek sales leads through advertising and promotion
They don't know the company	They are familiar with the company	Build prior awareness of the business with advertising
They don't need to buy	They need to buy	Identify the relevant clusters of people
They feel under pressure	They are helped to feel relaxed	Carry out the interview at a place and time that relaxes the prospect
They have no experience of buying the product or buying from the company	They or someone they know has bought the same product or from the same company	Existing customers are the best source of business. Referrals are also excellent sources of business
They don't understand the rewards that purchase will bring	They know why they should buy	Sell the benefits
There is no incentive to buy now	They feel they will lose out if they don't buy now	Encourage them to buy now rather than delay
They think other products or companies may be better	They believe that your product is the best	Tell the customer why to buy from your company

Table 15   **How to improve your chances of winning. Many of these points apply equally to love**

Services you could offer the customer

Free survey

Free design

Free technical advice

Free report on issues important to your customers

Loan of display equipment

Free training

Add your ideas here

Table 16 **Offering a customer an up-front, no commitment benefit is a good way to establish a link and understand more about the customer's needs**

Answer each question in Table 17 by ticking either the 'yes' or 'no' box.

The quiz shows that being a good lover and a good sales person is about putting effort into the relationship. It's about caring for the other person, and putting their needs before your own. You have to have a good knowledge of the needs of your lover and your customer. And you have to help them achieve those needs. As they achieve satisfaction, they will help you, too.

Your effort will pay off, because in the long run you'll have a better relationship and better sales results.

When you need emotional support, you have a lover who will help you. And when you need sales, the customer will give you the business rather than to a competitor.

Test your seductive powers

What kind of lover are you?			What kind of seller are you?		
	Yes	No		Yes	No
Do you know what sort of person would want to be your lover?	☐	☐	Do you know what sort of person would buy from you?	☐	☐
Do you know where to find a potential lover?	☐	☐	Do you know where to find potential customers?	☐	☐
Do you know how to make your potential lover relax?	☐	☐	Do you know how to get your prospect to relax?	☐	☐
Do you know your lover's interests, and share them?	☐	☐	Do you know your customers' interests and show an interest in them?	☐	☐
Do you understand your lover's needs?	☐	☐	Do you understand your customers' needs?	☐	☐
Do you take your lover to events your lover will enjoy?	☐	☐	Do you normally ask for the order?	☐	☐
Do you call your lover 'Darling' or a similar endearment?	☐	☐	Do you know the personal interests of your main customers?	☐	☐
Do you buy flowers (or similar presents)?	☐	☐	Do you normally get to your appointments on time?	☐	☐
Do you let your lover win arguments?	☐	☐	Do you prepare for each meeting?	☐	☐
Do you do the jobs your lover asks you to do?	☐	☐	Do you have an objective for each meeting?	☐	☐

Test your seductive powers (Cont.)

Do you know what satisfies your lover in bed?	☐	☐	Do you summarise the results after most meetings?	☐	☐
In bed, do you do the things your lover would like?	☐	☐	Do you avoid criticising your competitors?	☐	☐
Does your lover usually have an orgasm?	☐	☐	Do you have an excellent knowledge of your products?	☐	☐
Do you avoid situations which might lead to infidelity (for example going for singles bars)?	☐	☐	Do you have an excellent knowledge of your competitors' products?	☐	☐
Do you openly discuss personal problems with your lover?	☐	☐	Do you suggest marketing campaigns to your customers?	☐	☐
Do you share the housework evenly?	☐	☐	Do you keep in touch with major customers even when you aren't looking for an order?	☐	☐
Do you share income evenly?	☐	☐	Do you know all the companies where you might win sales?	☐	☐
Do you share assets (like house and car) evenly?	☐	☐	Do you liaise closely with other departments (such as technical or marketing)?	☐	☐
Do you know the christian name of your lover's grandmother?	☐	☐	Do you entertain your customer?	☐	☐
Do you bring your lover an early morning cup of tea or coffee?	☐	☐	Do you understand your customer's body language?	☐	☐
Total	☐	☐		☐	☐

How many 'Yes's' did you score? Now see how well you did by looking at the score card which follows.

The good lover, good seller scorecard	
As a lover	**As a seller**
up to 9 You need to spend more time understanding your lover's needs. Practise looking at things from your lover's point of view. The extra effort will give you a more rewarding life.	There are lots of things you can learn from this book. It could turn you into a seductive seller. Recognising your weaknesses is the first step to excellence.
10–15 You make efforts to care for your lover, but things like work sometimes get in the way. Try to set aside some special time to make your relationship more special.	You have mastered all the essential skills of selling. But you could put more thought into the planning and preparation of your work. It will help you stand out.
16–20 You are a considerate, caring human being, and your lover is a lucky person.	Congratulations. You are set to achieve great things in selling. It's only a matter of time.

Table 17 **The good lover, good seller quiz**

ACTION POINTS

♥ Avoid cold calling – it will depress you, it wastes your valuable time, and it doesn't work.

♥ Establish a link with the customer. This gives you reason to call him.

♥ Ensure that the customer is aware of you and ready to buy. Strategies to achieve this include getting sales leads.

♥ An indirect approach, offering a service, is a less threatening way to approach a customer.

♥ Seek to understand your lover and your customer, and put effort into the relationship.

Getting Through

As buyers demand long-term relationships, they are less likely to grant an interview without an appointment. Many types of selling have always required an appointment. Most requests for an interview are made by telephone, so this activity is an essential part of the seductive selling process.

Requesting an interview follows the same format as asking for a date. It is possibly the most nerve-racking part of selling. You have to pick up the phone, get past the secretary, and ask for a meeting. This is the start of the selling process. Table 18 indicates the five steps needed to getting a meeting, either with a lover or a customer.

The five steps to making an appointment or a date
1. Establish a rapport with the other person.
2. Discuss the other person's needs and interests.
3. Assess that the other person feels positive about taking the relationship to the next stage.
4. Ask for the interview.
5. Agree a date and time.

Table 18 **Fixing a meeting is the first positive step of the selling process**

These steps demonstrate that from the start you should be searching to understand the needs of the other person. Your style should be sympathetic, understanding and caring. And you have to listen sensitively to how the other person is responding to your words. Later we look at what you should say, and how to say it. But first we consider the problem of getting through to the buyer.

PREPARATION

The first stage in telesales is to discover the name and title of the right buyer. Phone and ask the telephonist, 'Who is responsible for car leasing?' When you get the person's name, check his title. Check the spelling, too. People get cross if you get their name wrong, and it will save time later on.

PHONING AT THE RIGHT TIME

One of the best times to ring is first thing in the morning, before the secretary arrives. The buyer will often answer his own phone.

John is the creative director of an advertising agency. He keeps a list of possible clients at his desk. When something good happens, like winning an account, he immediately phones the next prospect. His confidence and high spirits are infectious, and it often gets him a meeting with the prospect.

Keep trying

Experienced telesales people know that it can take six calls to reach a decision maker. So there is no point in getting discouraged after one, three or even five calls.

When you get through

Rules apply to telesales, just like any other sphere of business.

1. Tell the customer why you're calling. This should contain a benefit to the customer.

Six strategies for reaching the boss

How do you get through to the decision maker? Getting past the secretary isn't easy. She will often ask, 'What's it about?' Here are six ways to improve your chances.

1. You are more likely to get through if you have a link (which is discussed in Chapter 5). This gives you extra credibility. You might say, 'I met Mr Smith last week, and he asked me to call him'.
2. It is easier to get through if the buyer has responded to your advertising and promotion. You can say, 'He enquired about our office furniture last week. I wanted to discuss his needs with him'.
3. You can also adopt an indirect approach, which we discussed in Chapter 5. You could tell the secretary you want to personalise some information for him.
4. If the secretary says he is in a meeting, ask when the meeting should finish. Mentally add half an hour because meetings often over-run. Ring him back at that time.
5. If the secretary says he isn't available, ask her assistance. Say. 'Could you help me contact him?' When people are asked favours, they feel moved to help. Ask, 'When do you expect he will be free?'
6. Another good strategy is to get the secretary on your side. Include a benefit for her if possible. If you're selling office furniture, you can ask, 'How is the furniture in your office?'

Table 19 **Getting through to the decision maker**

2. Ask if you can go on. Most people say yes. Asking the customer's permission to continue is a powerful device. It gets the customer involved in the conversation early on. And by committing himself to continuing the conversation, he will listen more positively.
3. Keep the message simple. Use short words and short sentences.
4. Involve the listener. Ask questions and vary the pace.
5. Avoid 'sales techniques'. Ask directly for the business. If the listener says no, don't seek to change his mind. Don't con-

tinue a call where the customer doesn't want to buy. Thank the customer and finish the call.

6. Build a case by seeking the customer's agreement on major points, as in, 'Do you think it's important to have enough money to live comfortably when you retire?'

7. Listen to the person's voice. Become sensitised to changes in tone. Why is the customer becoming hesitant; why is there a hardening in her tone?

8. Vary your voice. Don't sound monotonous. Communicate the right emotions: interest, enthusiasm or even excitement.

9. Understand the customer's fears of dealing with an unknown business on the phone. See how you can overcome them. Can you mention some big firms who are customers? Can you quote case histories where you have saved the customer money? Are you a long established firm? Have you experience in the customer's industry?

10. At the end of the call, summarise the action you will take. This might mean recapping on the order details, or promising to ring back.

BLITZING THE CLIENT

One successful advertising agency, when asked to pitch for a new client's work, blitzes the client company.

Rather than having a meek introductory meeting, it mounts what it calls a 'file raiding party'. Several of the agency's executives visit the prospect's offices. They go to many different departments, get the views of staff, and photocopy many research documents and marketing figures. The prospective client is impressed by all this activity. It shows the level of energy and involvement that he can look forward to.

In the eventual presentation, the agency usually shows it has mastered the detail of the client's market and business – and it often wins the work.

ACTION POINTS

♥ Do your preparation before seeking an appointment. Find out who is the right person to contact.

♥ Decide your strategy for talking with the secretary.

♥ Consider phoning early or late to avoid the secretary.

♥ To reach a decision maker, you will have to make a sufficient number of calls.

♥ When you get through, structure the sales message to get the most out of the call. Seek involvement with the customer, and gain his agreement at each stage of the call.

Seductive Writing

There are many occasions when we have to write to a customer. Some of them are simple tasks, like confirming a meeting; others are more complex, such as writing a proposal document.

Let's take a simple letter, confirming an appointment. My company sends such letters out all the time. Here is an actual example:

Dear Mr. Jones

This is to confirm my arrangement to meet with you on Thursday 18th March at 12.00 noon at your office. I look forward to an interesting and informative discussion.

Yours sincerely

Kit Sadgrove

This is the worst letter you could send to anyone. It's as though you wrote a letter to your lover as follows:

Dear Alexandra

This is to confirm my arrangement to meet with you at your flat at 7.30pm on Thursday 18th March. I look forward to an interesting and informative discussion.

Yours sincerely

Kit Sadgrove

Both these letters are terse and unfeeling. They show little interest in the recipient. The customer won't look forward to meeting someone who writes such poor letters. He wants to see evidence that I care about him and his business. He wants to know that I can solve his problems. He also wants reassurance that I'm skilled; and this letter demonstrates none of these things. So let's re-write the letter, and try to show the customer we care about him.

Dear Mr. Jones

Thank you for giving me your time on the telephone today. I was interested to hear about the developments at Mega Corp; it is certainly a challenging time for you.

Thank you also for agreeing to see me at your offices at 12.00 noon on Thursday 18th March. I am greatly looking forward to making your acquaintance, and to learning more about Mega Corp.

In the meantime, we will be considering how we might be of assistance to you, and if you would like any help or information please don't hesitate to give me a ring.

With the rising costs of energy, you will be concerned to keep your fuel bills low; at the same time you don't want to invest in expensive plant which won't give you a payback.

Some companies in your industry are opting for more extensive metering; and this may be an option of interest to you. There are, however, many other ways of saving energy, and I will be interested in hearing what your next steps might be.

Thank you once again.

Yours sincerely

Kit Sadgrove

This letter is hardly more personalised than the first one; and using a word processor it will take no more time. Although it looks personal, most of the details are sufficiently standard to be suitable for all prospects.

Unlike the previous letter, this one talks about 'you', not 'I'. It looks at the issue from the customer's point of view. The new letter opens up a topic of discussion, and talks about the client's needs. It shows that I am interested only in the client's success. It indicates that we only want to help him, that we have no pre-conception about what he might want to buy; and that we are looking for information about his business.

This letter could even make the prospect look forward to the meeting. He might start the meeting by saying, 'I've been thinking about some of the things you talked about in your letter...'.

These concepts apply to all other forms of written communication to customers (whether direct mail, newsletter or advertisements). Use Table 20 to evaluate your written skills.

PREPARING A PROPOSAL

Whether you are offering a proposal of marriage or a proposal to build a sub-sea tunnel, the principles are the same: you are asking someone to accept your bid.

Does your business writing pass the seduction test?

Whatever you write to a customer should be as thoughtful as what you write to a lover. It should be:

- Personalised
- Detailed, comprehensive
- Focused on the reader
- Concerned
- Sincere
- Solution oriented

- Demonstrating skill or experience
- Friendly
- Open minded
- Honest, truthful

Table 20 **Writing to the customer**

All too often business proposals are strong on production information, weak on benefits, and completely lacking in warmth. Many proposals are written in a standard format, which looks like this:

- Background
- Objectives
- The brief
- Our response to the brief
- Method of work/strategy
- Benefits
- Staff involved
- Cost and timing
- Experience statement.

Yet a proposal should be more than a collection of facts and figures. It should reflect the fact that the two companies (you and your customer's) are run by people, and that your products are made by people. It should certainly not look as though it was put together by a computer. Ask the following questions:

- *What does the reader want to know?*
- *In what sequence does he want the information?*
- *How can we make our document look more attractive?*
- *How can we seem more friendly?*
- *How can we express our desire to work for the customer?*
- *How would we respond to a proposal like this?*
- *In what way could we make it look more professional?*

Answering these questions should lead you to write a better proposal.

FIVE TIPS FOR A BETTER PROPOSAL

1. **Sell the benefits**: Telling the reader the benefits are the most important part of the whole document. You should also tell the reader what he will miss if he *doesn't* buy.
2. **Specify the deliverables**: If you sell services, tell the customer what he will get. For example:

- The outcome will be the training of all senior management in TQM practice. This will include a complete set of course materials for each manager to take away.

or:

- The outcome will be a set of plans showing a re-designed ground floor sales area.

This is different from selling benefits. Here you are telling the customer exactly what he is getting for his money. Many proposals omit this point.

3. **Justify the price**: When I met a BP executive a while ago, he said, 'You'll have to say what will come out of this work. There has to be a financial benefit'. The best sort of proposal is a self financing one. You should try to show that your proposal will:

- reduce the client's costs
- increase the client's revenue
- improve the client's profit margin.

4. **Leave out the price**: Sometimes you can leave the price out altogether. If the client asks about the price, say, 'We can't price it until we've agreed the details of the project.' Leaving out the price helps to focus the client's mind on the service itself. Sometimes he becomes so keen to get the service that you can mention the price casually in the course of a meeting, and it gets passed without a quibble. This device works best with clients who know and trust you.

5. **Include a comparison chart**: If you feel you are the best choice to win the order, create a table showing your benefits. Invite the client to assess the competition against your attributes. This has the advantage of letting you determine the important features. Table 21 gives an example of this.

HOW TO WRITE A LOVE LETTER

We have got out of the habit of writing love letters. It may be inevitable, with more instant methods of communication such as the telephone. But the telephone can never replace that private

Features and benefits	GLOBAL Inc.	Competitors		
		A	B	C
Hand finished	✓			
Six layers of paint	✓			
Made from biodegradable materials	✓			
An ISO 9000 company	✓			
Substantial experience in your industry	✓			
Etc.				

Table 21 **Part of a competitor comparison table**

feeling when your loved one sits down to read your inner thoughts.

There is nothing more romantic than a love letter. A telephone conversation could never be wrapped in red ribbon and stored in the attic. Table 22 shows how to write a love letter.

How to write a love letter

1. Tell your lover something amusing or interesting about your day. Mention an incident over someone you met. Don't mention anyone of the opposite sex. Your lover is guaranteed to believe there is a rival.
2. Concentrate on things which you share knowledge of, or secrets known only to the two of you.
3. Say 'I love you'. Say 'I miss you'. This will be difficult if you haven't been brought up to express your emotions. But your lover will be waiting to hear you say the words.
4. State why you love your lover. What features is your lover most proud of? Is it the eyes, the dry humour, or the self-confident manner? Say that you miss it.
5. Tell your lover you're looking forward to meeting again soon.

Table 22 **The structure of a love letter**

GET INTO THE PRESS

Press coverage can produce the most astonishing results. **Safeclean**, a carpet cleaning company, got a mention in the *Daily Telegraph*. The company's telephones were besieged for days on end, and each of Safeclean's 80 franchisees won, on average, an extra £500 worth of work. From one small article, the company gained an extra £40 000 worth of work.

If you haven't gained publicity in your local media, now is the time to start. All you have to do is think up a newsworthy story, and write it in the form that the newspaper would use it (for example, 'Major order for peripherals'), and post it to the media. Remember to get your customer's approval.

A LITTLE, A LOT OF THE TIME

Lovers like constant reassurance that they are needed. Customers also need constant communication. If you stop communicating, nothing will happen for some time. But eventually your market share will begin to fall, as competitors begin to lure away your customers. Few customers need many words. Most have a reduced capacity for concentrating on the written word. They require small amounts of information. It's called **information snacking**. That doesn't mean to say that they won't read a lot about something they are interested in. But it does mean that the information must be broken up with lots of illustrations and graphics.

PUTTING ON THE STYLE

In some firms 'technical experts' rule. Here the literature is technically detailed but lacking in warmth and interest. The experts who produce this material see the reader as an architect or an engineer, not a human being. Yet these readers see the same magazines and the same television programmes as we do.

Some firms have broken the mould, and produced stunning

brochures filled with exquisite design and imaginative photography. These brochures, for lintels and bricks, have shown what can be done. Industrial markets are as competitive as any other, and it is important for your literature to stand out.

If your sales material is less than seductive, try to get it changed. Don't let the technical experts force you into accepting dull literature.

ACTION POINTS

♥ Check what standard letters are sent out. Avoid sending out terse and unfriendly letters.

♥ Make sure your letters are as knowledgeable, charming and customer-oriented as you yourself are.

♥ Assess whether your proposals meet the seduction test.

♥ Specify fully the benefits and deliverables in your proposal.

♥ Don't ignore the opportunity of free press coverage.

♥ Ensure that your sales literature is seductive.

Communicate fully

The Seduction Process

So far in *Seductive Selling*, we've assessed the market and located a customer. We've contacted the customer and we've made an appointment to see him. Now the moment of truth is approaching. It's time for the sales interview.

The sales interview is like going on a date. There are two reasons why people go on a date; men want sex and women want love. Happily, they manage to reconcile themselves to each other's needs. That is what's called a relationship.

Similarly, **there are only two reasons why a sales meeting takes place.** You want a sale, and the buyer wants to solve a problem.

That means the meeting is full of both conflict and desire. There is conflict because each side wants different things. The buyer wants to pay as little as possible. You want the reverse. There is also desire, because you need each other. You have a product he needs. He has the cash you want.

If you can put aside your differences, you can both win. You can develop a successful relationship based on mutual understanding and the satisfaction of each other's needs. If you can't reach an understanding, the buyer will do what all unhappy lovers do. He will seek a relationship with someone else. He will find another supplier.

Because the buyer has such different needs from you, and because you have to satisfy those needs, it is vital to have **empathy.**

Empathy is the ability to understand the buyer's position. It's being able to see the other's point of view. If you have empathy, it will reveal itself in the way you nod your head, the way you listen to the buyer's comments, and the way you sympathise with his difficulties. It will also reveal itself in the way you formulate your proposal, and the success with which it is received.

Bearing this in mind, we now look in detail at the seductive selling process itself.

THE SELLING PROCESS

Before the interview: the preparation phase

Sales people are often taught to have an objective for each meeting. This is good practice if it helps you reflect on what the customer may need and how you might help him. But you should not define in advance exactly what you will sell the customer: that can only be assessed in the meeting itself.

You should, however, have gathered as much information about the customer as possible in advance. This is a subject we examined in Chapter 3.

It helps to read the trade press or corporate newsletters in the customer's reception area. It will let you refer to a new product or an industry issue, and thereby demonstrate impressive knowledge.

In the interview: find out as much as you can about the client

Probe to understand his situation, his problem, or his strengths and weaknesses. This should take the majority of the time in the meeting. Don't rush to put your product on the table. It is best to wait until the client says, 'So how can your company help me?' This shows that his mind has turned to seeking a solution.

Find out exactly what he needs. When people are buying a house, they aren't buying bricks and rooms. Some are buying peace, some are seeking space, and others are buying status.

Define the customer's needs

It helps to have a formal brief from the customer, such as a tender document. You may need to sit down with the client and go through the document, clarifying the detail. It could be to your advantage to get the client to change his mind about the written brief. It means that the competitors will then be working to the old faulty brief.

Be careful, however, not to embarrass the customer. Excessive scrutiny of a document will usually reveal inconsistencies and exposing them may cause stress for the client.

Make a link between his need and your products

People don't always know why they want something. If you can demonstrate that your product fulfils their needs, you have won the sale.

You have to be careful about turning too quickly to your products, because it can look as though you have lost interest in the buyer. One way of creating a link between his needs and your product is by showing him that you have met similar situations before. More importantly, show that you have *solved* similar problems before.

Suggest a range of options

The options may include a review of what your competitors might offer. 'Plastic drains are cheap but they can rot and crack. Cast iron can rust and is heavy, and is difficult to join. Stainless steel is the option that suits your needs...' Here you are covertly attacking the opposition (but on a purely factual basis).

Sometimes the client may not be aware of the other options, and you will have to decide whether it is best to keep quiet and risk him finding out later; or mentioning them now and risk bringing them to his attention.

Recommend the best option

You will want to emphasise the benefits of using your product or service, and the disadvantages of delay. You need to watch the buyer's body language at this point. See whether he reacts positively. If he doesn't, halt the presentation, and get his views. Suggest how your product could help meet his need.

Get the customer's reaction

By now the customer will be bored of letting you talk. Now is the time to shut up. The client will want to air his views. *Note carefully any objection.*

Counter objections

You should be able to forecast and counter all the main objections to your products (and we look at these in more detail in Chapter 12).

You should then go back to the previous stage (to get the customer's reaction). If necessary, counter new objections. If you start to get buying signals (which we cover in Chapters 10 and 13), move to the next stage.

Close the sale

To win the sale, *all* the factors must be right. Don't be in too much of a hurry to close. Wait until the buyer gives clear signals that he wants to buy. We look at the close in more detail in Chapter 13. Meanwhile, Table 23 contains seven things to avoid in your presentation.

After the sale: follow up

Sales people always have to complete paperwork after a sales interview. Good record keeping is essential. Apart from completing the records required by your company, note any information which the buyer gave you. This might include news about his business, his family or his interests. It may be useful on your next meeting.

If you are seeking a high value sale, you should send a letter thanking the buyer for his time, and recalling the main points of the meeting. A partly standardised letter will save you time.

Seven things you should avoid in a sales presentation

- *Don't use jargon* – if the buyer doesn't understand what you're saying, he can't buy from you.
- *Don't use abstract ideas* – if you use words like 'high quality', the buyer may think you mean 'expensive' or 'over-engineered'. Use concrete words and benefits, and make your words match the customer's needs.
- *Don't offer a leaflet instead of selling* – if you show a buyer a leaflet with lots of copy, he may offer to read it later. This will delay the decision. Don't allow him to avoid saying 'yes' or 'no'. Equally, don't say to the buyer, 'It's all in the leaflet'. This is using a leaflet as a substitute for selling. Many top sales people never show a leaflet.
- *Don't take out your product as soon as you meet the client* – A customer may have many things he wants to say when he meets you. Give him the time to say them. It may feel like a waste of time, but it is a necessary part of the process. This doesn't mean letting the buyer ramble on about his holidays. Once the meeting is under way, keep the customer focused on the right subject.
- *Don't ignore his opinions or needs* – The customer may be misguided but he is never wrong. Different clients tackle the same problem with different solutions, each of which may be right for them. The customer often knows what will be acceptable inside his company.
- *Don't use a fixed sales talk* – This is like deciding in advance what you will sell the customer. No one has a product so standardised that it can't be packaged differently to meet different clients' needs. A fixed sales talk tells the customer that you don't see him as an individual. It tells him you aren't interested in his special requirements.
- *Don't try to close too early* – It is frustrating when a prospect dithers or talks excessively. But restrain yourself from saying, 'Look, do you want it or not?' The client will show you by words and gestures (Chapter 10) when he is ready to buy.

Table 23 **How to avoid losing a sale**

HOW DO YOUR CUSTOMERS FEEL ABOUT THEIR PURCHASE?

There are four main types of purchases, shown in Table 24.

Some products are *grudge purchases*. They are things we have to buy, but which give us no perceived benefit. Petrol and tyres are two examples.

Convenience shopping is when you go into a supermarket or corner shop to buy routine items. You are not emotionally involved with the products.

Comparison shopping is when you buy a big ticket item, and you compare the prices and performance of different products in different shops.

Enjoyment shopping is for pleasure. The purchase could be for the purchaser or it could be a gift for someone else; but it is a relaxed, pleasant activity.

There are equivalents in love to the four categories of purchasing. The *Grudge* category is where a prostitute participates in a loveless sex. *Convenience* sex is the type that some couples in long-standing relationships have – it is routine. *Comparison* sex is certainly common – we all wonder what sort of lover different

Types of purchasing			
Emotion	Category	Typical purchase	The lover's equivalent
Lack of pleasure ▲	Grudge	Petrol	Prostitution
	Convenience	Groceries	Convenience
	Comparison	Hi-fi	Comparison
▼ *Pleasure*	Enjoyment	Jewellery	Active participation or initiation

Table 24 **The four categories of purchase**

people might make. The *Enjoyment* category involves active sexual involvement, and is found both in a secure long-term relationship and at the start of a new affair.

KNOWING YOUR PRODUCT

Product knowledge is vital in selling. You can't understand the features and benefits of your product if you don't understand how it works. Formal training is invaluable. It's like learning to drive a car. If you are formally shown how to do something, it gives you extra confidence and professionalism. You may need to go on a product knowledge course. At the very least, go and visit your technical department, and ask them some detailed questions. Get them to take the product apart.

An advertising agency boss came back from a client meeting in an angry yet elated state. The agency had to prepare an advertising campaign for a Philips lady's electric shaver. He had asked the marketing department whether the shaver had any special features. The department said there were none. At a chance meeting with a technical manager, he asked the same question. The technical manager told him that the shaver ran at twice the speed of normal shavers, and this gave a smoother, safer cut. This led to an outstanding advertising campaign, based on an understanding of the product's technical features.

HOW TO SELL A COMMODITY PRODUCT

A commodity is a product that can't be distinguished from its competitors. Typical commodities are gold, cocoa and wheat. Many household products have become virtual commodities, too. Can the consumer *really* tell the difference between one brand of rice and another? Between the meat sold in one shop and another? Can she tell the difference between one brand of toothpaste and another?

The fewer distinguishing marks, the more that emotion comes into play. TV commercials seek to give an identity to otherwise anonymous cans of soft drink or packets of crisps.

For the buyer, there is rarely a clear choice. If there was, everyone would drive a Toyota, buy a Bosch fridge or buy Shell petrol. The fact that many brands exist shows that buyers have a range of needs.

Differentiate your product

You can differentiate your brand through your personality. A customer may buy your telephone equipment if he gets on better with you. Customer service, on-time delivery and other factors will be just as important to him as the technical features of the product. Table 25 suggests some ways to escape the commodity trap.

Ways of differentiating your product in selling
Get the marketing department to build added value into your product
Assess what issues are important to the customer (such as delivery or quality assurance), and seek to deliver that.
Show more understanding of the customer's needs
Be punctual
Give him industry news
Do helpful jobs for him
Provide free samples
Do the things you say you'll do
Be neater and smarter
Be nicer to his staff
Provide a better service for credit notes, or the picking up of faulty material
Provide written confirmation of orders, and minutes of meetings
Provide entertainment
Provide incentives (if this is legal or appropriate in your industry)

Table 25 **Avoiding the commodity trap**

The same applies in love. Our physical differences are not great. We have broadly similar features and abilities. It is the way that you care for someone that will win you a lover.

USING SALES PRESENTERS

Some sales people deride sales presenters – they prefer to chat informally to the customer, and find a presenter is inhibiting.

The truth is that we absorb much of our information through our eyes, and much less through our ears. Therefore a message which contains both sound *and* pictures will be more effective. The sales presenter acts as a focus, and serves to control the meeting.

Sales presenters don't have to be professionally produced. One very successful sales person habitually draws a five-pointed star. Clients are always impressed by this elegant shape, and they listen with bated breath as he uses each point to highlight a benefit.

You don't have to be five-star expert. Just draw a simple triangle on a sheet of paper, and watch the customer's eye get drawn to the sheet. The three points of the triangle allow you to make three observations.

In Table 26 is a list of other sales aids, with a blank box for you to add sales aids you can use.

THE DEMONSTRATION

Some sales people treat their product casually. They throw it on to the buyer's table in an offhand manner. They think it makes them look sophisticated or casual. But this behaviour tells the buyer that the sales person has little respect for his product. If you don't respect the product, why should he buy it?

Every Mars sales person has a small satin-lined wooden box. If he needs to give away a sample of the product, or show the different sizes available, he rests the product inside the box on its satin lining before showing it to the customer.

There the product sits in state, like a jewel on a cushion, on

Typical sales aids	Sales aids you can use
The product itself	
Swatches and colours	
Samples of the product	
Drawing of installations	
Photos of the product	
Brochures	
Corporate video	

Table 26 **Making maximum use of sales aids**

display to the customer. It may sound hammy, but it shows that the product should be treated with respect. And I never saw a buyer react with anything but respect towards the satin box.

Demonstrations also work for industrial products. The Managing Director of a road marking firm visits prospective companies. He meets the Managing Director, and takes him to the corporate car park. Then he asks him where he likes to park his car. There and then he marks out a spot, and labels it 'Managing Director'. The Managing Director is often so impressed with the speed and simplicity of the demonstration, and pleased with his exclusive car space, that he places the order while still in the car park.

SAMPLES

Your lover likes getting presents. It shows you care. The consumer likes getting presents, too. Samples are rarely mentioned in marketing books – perhaps the authors feel samples aren't important enough. But according to research by RSGB, two-thirds of consumers have bought a product outside their normal choice following the delivery of a free sample.

In other words, free samples are hugely powerful. The survey, carried out for Circular Distributors, says that consumers like samples because they take the risk out of purchasing new products. Seventy-nine per cent say that they find samples useful, compared with 40 per cent who say the same for advertising. Free samples are more powerful than advertising in persuading consumers to try new products.

Ensure you have samples to give away, no matter what you sell. Your sample might be a free design, a free assessment or a free trial period.

THE SALES PRESENTATION

You may have to make a big, formal presentation in front of an assembled audience. A major job may depend on your performance. If so, it is worth spending time preparing it.

The presentation will be similar in many ways to a basic sales call. But there will be less dialogue and it will be more structured, with formal presentations, questions and answers.

Involve the client

Many companies make the mistake of treating the client as the passive recipient of your information. The client is judging the personal chemistry between the presenter and himself just as much as he is evaluating the technical or creative excellence of your proposals.

The best presentations involve the customer. There are many ways to do this, for example:

- Ask the audience to give their names.
- Ask them rhetorical questions.
- Get them to do something physical, such as holding a drawing.
- Involve them in a role play.
- Tell them to ask questions whenever they want. It is a mistake to tell the client to hold questions to the end. Your audience is not a group of children. They expect to participate. It is, after all, their money.

Respond positively to all questions. Flatter the questioner by telling him 'That's an important question.' You don't need to have all the answers. The customer will be proud to have asked a question which needs such careful thought that you need to find out the answer later and get back to him. Many clients like to feel superior, and if you glibly answer every question, you defeat them.

In Table 27 are important points for delivering a better formal presentation.

Five points for a winning presentation

1. **Rehearse beforehand in front of a mirror** – Check that you aren't nervously shaking your papers, or that your body language expresses anxiety.
2. **Focus on the client, not your own organisation** – The first slide should *never* be headed, 'About us'. It should relate to the client.
3. **Watch the decision maker** among the audience (perhaps the Chief Executive). His body language will tell you how well you are doing.
4. **Use professional and effective visual aids** – Use the type which you feel most relaxed with, whether slides, overhead slides, flip chart, or computer-based presentation scheme.
5. **Have a beginning, a middle and an end** – Remember the old saying: 'Tell them what you're going to say. Say it. Then tell them what you said'.

Table 27 **These points are often overlooked by presenters**

THE STRUCTURE OF THE BIG PRESENTATION

As mentioned earlier, the presentation may resemble an ordinary sales call, except that it is more formally structured. But there are specific differences, especially in the way that you close the meeting.

The presentation is likely to have the following format:

1. *Outline the customer's situation; focus on his problem*
   Show the customer that you understand his market or problem. This will build his trust, and help him relax. In many

sales situations, understanding the market or the customer's problem is the most important criterion. Show that you empathise with his situation.

2. *Suggest options available to him*
Exploring options allows you to forestall objections. It also shows that you have made a considered judgement after reviewing all the evidence.

3. *Recommend the best option*
This is the highlight of the presentation. It is the part that the client has been waiting for. Present it as dramatically and professionally as your budget allows. Tell the client the benefits that your proposal will bring.

4. *Gain the customer's reaction to the proposal and counter objections*
The customer may start asking questions at this stage, or raising objections. Try to distinguish between a customer who is talking for the sake of exercising his authority, and one who has serious reservations about your proposal.

5. *Convert the meeting into a social event*
In a presentation, you aren't likely to close the sale. The customer may have other presentations to see. And he will want to confer with his colleagues in private. But you should create a social event (if only coffee) after the presentation. This will let you get close to the customer's team, build a rapport, and assess the customer's response to the presentation.

Listed in this way, the process can seem dry. But your presentation should be anything but dry. This is a subject which we turn to next.

PUTTING ON A STRIP SHOW

A presentation is like a strip show. The audience is seated around you, and you are on your feet. The audience are expectant. They want you to reveal yourself.

A stripper could give you hints about how to manage a sales presentation. Strippers know that delay and concealment is more interesting than bare facts. They know that the imagination is as powerful a force as anything that can be seen in the flesh. The longer the suspense, the more excited the audience gets. They create customer involvement by moving among the audience. They keep the best until last. They build to a climax. The lights go off. There is a roar of applause.

For a sales presentation, there are many lessons to be learnt:

- Don't reveal your ideas until you have wound the audience into a state of excitement.
- Involve your audience by asking them rhetorical questions, talking about their experiences, or even moving among them.
- Use the technology of lights and pictures to build emotion and drama.
- Always keep in mind that you are on a stage. Talk slowly and clearly. Use effective hand gestures and body language.

Remember that you are creating an impression. You are not selling them a new incinerator; you are solving their smelly, dangerous and illegal refuse storage problem. In its place you are creating a haven, where the sun always shines and the problems of garbage are magicked away.

Remember that your presentation has to be dramatic. Each stage of the presentation represents another veil being whipped away. With each veil, the audience should cry 'Yes!' They should demand, 'More!'

THE EXHIBITION

Another place where seductive selling takes place is an exhibition hall. Stands at an exhibition are like sex shops in the red light district in Hamburg. Tourists wander slowly down the seedy streets looking to left and right, deciding which strip show is the most attractive. From the lighted windows, prostitutes gaze on the passers-by, or call to them.

At the exhibition, you should make your stand the most desirable – the one which brings all the visitors flocking. To make your stand attractive, you have to follow some simple rules.

- Don't stand at the entrance to your stand, like a doorman outside a strip club waiting to pounce on passers-by.
- Design your stand so that it stands out. Make sure the headline graphics can be read at a distance of six metres.
- Make sure that the stand communicates the word 'new'. If you have no new products, show new applications or new case histories. Show how your products make life easy, make money, or increase prestige.
- Make sure that people can get on and off your stand without feeling trapped. Reduce the emotional commitment required in coming on to your stand.
- Make people want to learn more. Show a video or put on a demonstration. Involve visitors by giving them a challenge or asking them to try a new product.

AFTER THE EXHIBITION

The end of an exhibition is like the end of a first date. After the date, you have your friend's name and telephone number in your pocket. But how well did you do on the date? Did you arouse any interest?

You have to ring up and ask for another date. If you get a positive response, this could be the start of a long-term relationship.

Most exhibitors are skilled about collecting visitors' business cards. They are less skilled at contacting the visitors after the exhibition. The information should be handed over to a telesales person, and a strategy devised. Do you want to seek appointments, or to sell them your product over the telephone?

Most of the names you collect at an exhibition will not result in any business. But a few will become important new customers, if you follow them up.

ACTION POINTS

♥ Remember that a sales meeting takes place because a buyer wants something. It is up to you to help him define that want, and translate it into an order.

♥ Understand at least in broad terms what you expect to get out of the sales meeting.

♥ Things to avoid in a presentation include jargon, abstract ideas, and failure to listen to the customer.

♥ If you don't fully understand your product, you will be at a major disadvantage.

♥ You can differentiate your product through selling, even in a commodity market.

♥ Use a sales presenter, demonstration and samples whenever possible.

♥ In a formal presentation, involve the customer. Focus on his needs, not your capabilities.

♥ Exhibitions can be made more effective by making your stand more seductive. Follow up your leads afterwards.

9

Building a Relationship

In this chapter, we look at ways of building a relationship, starting with the characteristics you need to be a perfect lover or seller. Then we look at buyer's limitations, whether imposed from outside or from within. Finally, we consider how to manage your relationships through a powerful tool called **Transactional Analysis**.

WHAT THEY NEED FROM YOU

Your effectiveness as a lover and a seller depends on many characteristics. They are listed in Table 28. Tick the boxes which apply to you. If some boxes remain empty, those are the ones to concentrate on.

UNDERSTANDING THE BUYER'S LIMITATIONS

If the buyer is reluctant to buy, it may be because he is unable to buy. This could be for one of several reasons, outlined in Table 29. Identifying the constraints will lead you to the answers.

The eight attributes for a perfect relationship

The way you behave ...	Towards your lover	(✓)	Towards your customer	(✓)
Understanding	You understand your lover's different moods, and what causes them	☐	You have an instinctive feel for a customer's motives and needs	☐
Knowledgeable	You know how to maintain an even relationship with your lover	☐	You know your products, and those of your competitors	☐
Responsive	You react quickly to changing circumstances to rectify problems	☐	You react to the changing requirements of the market and the customer	☐
Effective	You take action to improve the relationship	☐	You process work efficiently	☐
A communicator	You can express your feelings in a way that helps your lover to understand your needs	☐	You keep the customer up to date on matters of importance	☐
Courteous	You behave in a considerate way which is neither patronising nor aggressive	☐	You behave in a professional way towards the buyer	☐
Credible	Your lover trusts you through experience and shared problem solving	☐	You display confidence towards the buyer, and your relationship is built on trust and mutual understanding	☐
Caring	You want the best for your lover	☐	You want the best for your customer	☐

Table 28 **The characteristics of a lover and a seller are similar. Which aspects do you want to improve?**

Four constraints – and how to overcome them	
Constraint	**Solution**
1. The buyer may have to defer to a boss or a purchasing department.	Involve the boss or purchasing department. Ask for a joint meeting.
2. The buyer may not be able to buy items over a certain value.	Divide the product into chunks which he can buy on his own authority.
3. Corporate policy may require him to buy from another division of his company.	Find out if this division could buy from you. Or prove that the other division cannot supply the right product, at the right time or the right price.
4. He may be required to buy from approved suppliers.	Seek to become an approved supplier.

Table 29 **Understanding and resolving the buyer's limitations**

GAMES CUSTOMERS PLAY

Sometimes a customer is constrained from placing an order, not because of the external forces that we saw above, but due to forces inside the buyer himself. This is where customers start playing games. Sometimes they want you to demonstrate that you need them – just like a lover. To do this, they play the same sort of games that a lover plays.

Acting disinterested: A customer may take phone calls, or accept interruptions, while you are talking to him. This may be out of ignorance, or because he doesn't want you to think he is very interested in your products.

Playing hard to get: A customer may avoid giving you the order until the last possible minute, in order to keep you hanging on.

It's like agreeing to sex; the buyer's power over you is greatest only as long as he withholds the order.

One buyer puts a letter from Shell on his desk when a BP representative calls. When a Shell rep calls, he puts a BP or Exxon letter on the desk. He does this to make his suppliers unsure of themselves.

Emotional blackmail: A buyer may ask you what you are going to do for him in return for an order. Sometimes, he needs the sales person to show gratitude. It is understandable – the buyer feels he should get something out of the deal. In some countries, this kind of demand amounts to bribery – a very different situation from the buyer simply needing reassurance. Below we discuss ways of avoiding these kind of games, which are unprofessional and favour the buyer.

GAIN AN EDGE BY UNDERSTANDING YOUR RELATIONSHIPS BETTER

If you and your lover have a positive attitude towards each other, you'll have an effective relationship. Anything less than that means you become destructive or waste time playing games.

The same applies in selling. If you don't have a mature relationship with your customer, you won't earn his respect. But it goes further than that. In an age when product differences are slight, a superior customer relationship can win the sale.

Many products are very similar. One computer is like another and one hotel is like another. Temporary advantages gained by a technological advance are quickly matched. *That makes the skills and personality of the seller very important.*

You can be more effective at selling if you understand the relationship you have with your customer. By managing that relationship in a positive way, you will impress the customer and win his respect.

As more companies recognise they are in a 'people' business, they are increasingly turning to **Transactional Analysis** (TA). This reveals the benefits of having a positive relationship with others. It works for lovers, too.

In TA, there are three types of people:

1. the Parent
2. the Child
3. the Adult.

Which role do you play?

The Parent: The parent is the worst kind of Victorian parent you could imagine. He feels superior and condescending to those around him. He is full of repressed anger. He treats others as children. He is quick to find blame. He is a bully. He issues orders. He is critical.

People in positions of minor power, like some buyers, can adopt this attitude. They say, 'I haven't possibly got time to see you... Your last order was delivered very late... Why can't your range be as good as your competitors?...'.

A male lover adopting a Parent state will say, 'Why can't you keep the house neater?... This food is awful...' A female Parent will say, 'Why can't you earn as much money as he does next door?...' (The Parent uses the word 'You' a lot.)

The Child: This is the voice of the spoilt and insecure child. He can be sulky, timid and demanding. He expects to receive without giving. Thwarted lovers can display this state. They say things like, 'If you really loved me, you would do that for me.' (They use the word 'me' a lot.) If he dared, the Child sales person would say, 'That's not a very big order.'

The Adult: The adult is essentially calm. He seeks to bring out the Adult in other people. He collaborates well, and treats people as equals. He spends much of his time resolving problems. The Adult state is found in people who are in control of their own lives. People with real power display an Adult state. They don't need to prove themselves; and to achieve their goals they get those around them to work as a team. They tend to ask questions like, 'How can we resolve this problem?' (The Adult uses the word 'We' a lot.)

The five relationships

There are five main relationships that you can have with others. These are shown in Table 30.

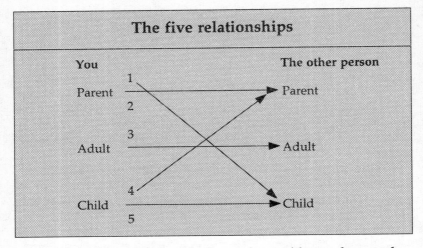

Table 30 **Which relationship do you have with your lover and your customer?**

The three most common relationships are as follows:

Parent → Child: This is the attitude a bank manager adopts when talking to an overdrawn customer. For anyone in sales, it is a condescending approach. The sales person thinks he knows more than the customer. He says, 'Well I can't help you if you don't know what you want.' Sales people who work in a retail outlet (a fixed point to which customers come) are more likely to adopt a Parent state.

Child → Parent: This is the salesman wheedling for an order. The sales person tries to flatter the customer in a insincere way. An angry customer who shouts, waves his arms about, uses abusive language and doesn't stick to the point, is also in a Child state.

Adult → Adult: This is the best approach. As a lover, you treat your partner as a mature adult. You say what you think, but you avoid destructive comment. In selling, you treat your customer as an equal, seeking to understand his needs, and seeing how both of you can win. You avoid emotional blackmail or sales tricks.

Generally Adults have relationships with other Adults. This is because the Adult seeks to bring out the Adult in the other person. As an Adult, you may often find yourself dealing with a buyer who behaves like a Parent. You should be able, because of your maturity and personality, to bring him round to behaving like another Adult.

The buyer may revert to a Parent state with his staff and other

Find out what sort of relationship you have		
Which of these words describe your attitude...	towards your lover? ✓	towards your customer? ✓
1. Diffident		
2. Condescending		
3. Critical		
4. Caring		
5. Dependent		
6. Supportive		
7. Emotional		
8. Rational		
9. Understanding		
10. Pedantic		
11. Insecure		
12. Superior		

Table 31   **Do you have a Child, Parent, or Adult relationship with your lover or customer?**

sales people ('When will you ever learn, Michael?') This is because the staff adopt a Child state towards him, and he reinforces it. Each time you re-visit this buyer, he may be in his Parent state. You will have to assert yourself, and encourage him to adopt an Adult state.

Sometimes you may treat people as one Adult to another, but they respond like a Parent to a Child. When this happens, try to keep the conversation on an Adult level. It is tempting, but wrong, to snap back childishly. Try to recognise when someone is 'hooking' your Child or Parent state. Pause before you reply. Give your Adult state time to come to the fore.

WORKING OUT WHO YOU ARE

What words would you use to describe your relationship with your lover and your customers? Tick the boxes in Table 31 (page 91) which apply to you.

How to score your answers:
Score one Child point for each tick in box 1, 5, 7 or 11.
Score one Parent point for each tick in box 2, 3, 10 or 12.
Score one Adult point for each tick in box 4, 6, 8 or 9.

Put your total scores in the boxes below.

Your relationship with your lover			Your relationship with your customer		
Child points	Parent points	Adult points	Child points	Parent points	Adult points

See what action you should take to improve your relationships. Maybe you should be more caring, less demanding, or more self-assertive? Decide what steps you can take to adopt a Child or

Parent state less often. See how you can boost your Adult state. Table 32 in the next section offers some suggestions.

USING TRANSACTIONAL ANALYSIS (TA) TO SELL

Many people initially find TA a little strange. But if you seek to understand the benefits it can bring, you'll become even more successful as a sales person. Use TA in some of your visits, and see if it works. The fact that you're reading this book shows that you're alert to new ideas. Here is how to use TA:

- Understand your goals and ambitions, and how you can achieve them. If you want an order, how will you get it?
- Work out what state the buyer is in. If he is in a Child or Parent state, try to work out why that is.
- Emphasise positive solutions. If the buyer says 'We can't afford it', find out why that is. Adults are able to discuss money and problems without embarrassment.
- Seek the buyer's help in arriving at a solution. Ask his advice.
- Don't get sidetracked. If the buyer tries to play games, make personal attacks, or gossip, accept the point and then continue towards your objective. Don't get lured into a pointless and distracting argument.

To prove that TA works, read the first paragraph of this section again ('Many people initially...'). That paragraph uses many TA devices (specifically items 1, 4, 5 and 7 of Table 32); but it seemed quite normal to you, didn't it?

Eleven ways to manage your relationships using TA

1. Ask for what you want – be politely assertive
2. Ask for help in the relationship. Say 'I need you'. People want to feel needed. Even in large cities like Madrid or Bonn, people try to help a stranger who says, 'Could you tell me how to get to . . .'
3. Put emotion into the relationship; disclose something about yourself
4. Counter a negative point with a positive point.
5. Reward people by giving them attention and recognition.
6. Share apprehension: don't repress it.
7. Think well of people. Assume they want to succeed; it is merely circumstances which prevent them from adopting an Adult state. Encourage people to take responsibility.
8. Allow people to save face. Don't force them into humiliating admissions.
9. Help people to recognise the effects of their negative behaviour.
10. Acknowledge weakness. If you (or your business) deserve blame, accept it. But don't dwell on it. And look to the future. Ask, 'What can we do to ensure that this doesn't happen in the future?'
11. Count to ten before you respond to negative behaviour. It will stop you from responding in a Child or Parent state.

Table 32 **The secrets of Transactional Analysis**

ACTION POINTS

♥ Assess whether you lack any of the attributes needed for a perfect relationship. Work on your weaknesses.

♥ Understand the buyer's limitations. See how you can free him from them.

♥ Be aware of the games the buyer plays. Be ready to counter them or avoid them.

♥ Recognise that your relationship with the customer may be the deciding factor in wining business, and seek to manage that relationship.

♥ See how you can reduce the amount of time you spend in a Child or Parent state. Seek to have an Adult-Adult relationship with the customer.

Use Your Body

The opposite sex will make up their mind about you in three minutes. So will the buyer. They may hardly listen to *what* you are saying; but they will listen to *how* you say it. They will take in your posture, movement and gaze, and a host of small details, while hardly being aware of it.

If you want to make a conquest, whether in love or in selling, you have just three minutes to do it. Table 33 contains guidelines for that all-important first meeting.

BODY LANGUAGE

Men and women give out silent signals which show how they are feeling. This body language, which is unintentional, expresses many moods – anger, anxiety or boredom; hostility, arrogance or desire.

Understanding their moods will give you more power over them. It will make you more successful in sex and selling. First we look at the signs that reveal sexual attraction in Table 34.

But people often *aren't* interested in love. Table 35 reveals the gestures that should dissuade you from making an advance.

Few sales managers teach their sales force to understand body language. But an understanding of body language is useful for two purposes:

1. It helps you understand the customer's emotions. Body language can reveal when the buyer is unconvinced, thoughtful,

Seven ways to make the right impression

Meeting the buyer	Meeting your lover
1. Ensure your appearance is neat and that it conforms to his expectations of a reputable supplier (nothing too outlandish)	Ensure you look the part. Look like the person your partner would want to be seen with
2. Make your handshake firm (but not bone crushing)	Greet in the appropriate way – neither too reserved nor seeming to be a groper
3. Keep your gaze steadily on the buyer. Don't look shiftily at the floor or ceiling	Keep your gaze steadily on the person you are meeting
4. Emphasise your points with calm but not over-extravagant hand gestures	Emphasise your points with calm but not over-extravagant hand gestures
5. Ask questions which show an understanding and an interest in his business. It will make you seem a better conversationalist	Ask questions which show an interest in your partner. It will make you seem a better conversationalist
6. Try to be relaxed but businesslike. Humour can break the ice	Try to be relaxed but not too intense. Laughter can be an aphrodisiac
7. Show good manners. Don't sit down until invited. Don't lounge back	Show good manners. Old fashioned courtesy and charm can be attractive because they indicate your interest in your partner

Table 33 **First impressions count**

The tell-tale signs of love

- Points body or foot points towards the person desired.
- Touches own clothing; fingers hair or thigh. Straightens tie.
- Hooks fingers near the crotch (for example in belt).
- Puts hands on hips.
- Maintains steady eye contact.
- Pupils of the eye enlarge.
- Touches the person desired (for example to remove dust from jacket or to straighten his tie).
- Exposes wrists or palms.
- Crosses and uncrosses legs.
- Tilts head to one side.
- Moves closer to the desired person, or leans towards him.
- Parts legs, exposing crotch area when wearing trousers.
- Fondles a cylindrical object, such as a wine glass (woman).
- Tosses head, flicking hair away from face and shoulders (woman).

Table 34 **How people reveal their desire**

When the other person isn't in the mood

- Folds arms in front
- Clasps hands together
- Leans away from you
- Avoids eye contact
- Holds head down
- Keeps knees together

Table 35 **Six telling signs that show you aren't succeeding**

or ready to buy. It can tell the sales person how to respond more accurately to the buyer's mood.

2. It lets you radiate the right signals. A sales person should be seen to be relaxed, confident and friendly. Body language can help to express those feelings.

You have to look for a cluster of signals – a single gesture may be misleading.

Recently, I met a Quality Assurance Manager who displayed contradictory signals. He kept his arms folded firmly across his chest. But at the same time he was leaning forward and asking questions about the price. This told me he was unsure of himself, yet he was keen on what I was offering.

In Table 36 are the ten emotions that buyers express by gesture, and the strategies you should adopt to gain a sale.

SEVEN WAYS TO USE BODY LANGUAGE TO SELL

1. **Mimic his body posture**: Subordinates tend to reflect their superior's body posture. To make yourself more readily accepted by the buyer, you should try to match his body posture. If he rests one hand on the desk, you should do the same. But don't mimic hostile gestures – that isn't going to help your cause. If the buyer starts adopting *your* gestures, you're on course for a sale.

2. **Persuade the buyer to change his attitude**: There is no point in trying to clinch a sale to a buyer whose body language says he is bored, defensive or hostile.

   Your task is to get the buyer to adopt a set of positive gestures – those described in Table 36 as Honest, Interested and Ready to Buy.

3. **Don't invade the buyer's office**: You should avoid entering the buyer's territory without his permission. Allow him to enter his office first. Do not sit down until he gestures you to do so. Do not put your papers on his desk without asking permission. Do not rest your arms on his desk.

   Some buyers have a second table which they use for meetings. The buyer will feel less territorial about this desk, which means you can feel more relaxed about making use of it. The same applies when a buyer uses a meeting room for the interview. But although the table or meeting room is more neutral territory, avoid looking as though you own the place. You are still in the buyer's premises.

4. **Don't sit in opposition**: Avoid sitting directly opposite the buyer. This makes him feel you are confronting him. The best place is at right angles to him. This means you will sit at the next side of the table to him, with both of you sharing the same corner. This will allow the customer to look straight ahead without having to stare you in the face.

5. **Sit alongside the buyer**: With a customer you know well, you can sit on the same side of the table as him. This technique should be used with caution – he may feel you are being overly familiar. Seek his permission before you move round the table. Allow him enough space.

   Sitting on the buyer's side is useful when you need to review a chart or document with him. It also tells the buyer that you feel part of his team – you are both literally on the same side.

6. **Sit at the right height**: Avoid sitting in a chair that is higher than the buyer. If the chair height is adjustable, lower it. The buyer will feel more comfortable if he is literally superior to you. If you are in a negotiating position, you may want to sit at the same height.

7. **Take care when dealing with more than one buyer at once**: Where you meet two or more buyers at once, you should watch to see how they behave. Often the person with authority to buy holds the meeting in his office. By being behind the desk and by virtue of seniority, he becomes the focal point.

   Be careful to involve everyone at the meeting, especially those who seem to have buying power. At a meeting I attended recently with an oil company, one member of the customer's team started displaying 'bored' gestures. Knowing that he had the power to prevent the sale, I started asking him questions. As he started to answer the questions, he became more involved in the meeting again. He leant forward and ceased toying with his pen.

Ten emotions a buyer can express by body language

Buyer's emotion	Body language	How you should respond
Angry or frustrated	Eases collar away from neck, as though it is too tight	Stop selling; allow the buyer to explain his emotion
	Scratches the back of his neck	
Hostile or defensive	He sits back in his chair	Find out what is upsetting the buyer. Seek to overcome his objections
	He crosses his arms across his chest	
	Joins his hands	
	He crosses his legs	
Bored	Leans back	Stop talking. Involve the buyer more. Get him talking about himself and his company
	With elbow on table, he rests the weight of his head on his hand	
	Fiddles with objects	
	Flicks dust or hair off his clothes	
Arrogant or superior	Puts his hands behind his head	Grit your teeth. Keep your temper. Seek to involve him more by asking questions which will stir his emotions. 'How would this affect your position in the company?'. 'What sort of company is this?' 'How will the company have changed in a couple of years' time?'
	Tilts his chair back	
	Places the tips of his fingers together	
	Clasps hands behind back	
	Hands on hips	

Table 36 **Body language**

Ten emotions a buyer can express by body language (Cont.)		
Honest	Shows palms by opening his hands towards the listener	Seek his cooperation in moving towards a sale
Lying	Touches nose briefly Rubs eye Covers mouth momentarily	Probe to find the problem. Beware of putting too much trust in the buyer
Interested: ready for action	The buyer leans forward Tilts head to one side	Ask for the order (but check first that he isn't just ready to end the meeting – see below)
Evaluating your proposal	The buyer puts his hand to his cheek Strokes or massages his chin or lips	Give him time to think. See if he changes to 'Hostile', 'Ready to Buy', or 'Ready to End meeting' gestures
Ready to buy	Displays 'Interested' and 'Evaluating' gestures. Then leans forward expectantly	Ask for the order
Ready to end meeting without buying	Displays 'Bored' or 'Hostile' gestures; then leans forward expectantly	Terminate meeting without asking for the order

DRESSED FOR THE PART

What clothes do you wear to impress a lover? A sharp suit? Jeans and T shirt? Your clothes say a lot about you. They send a message to the world – I'm rich, I'm fashionable, I'm available or I'm strong. Changing your clothes can make you more attractive to the other sex. Find out what they would like to see you wearing. It might not be what you would choose. But you'll be surprised at how much sexier they'll find you.

Lovers buy an overall package when they choose to go with someone. And for the buyer, you personify your entire company. When he buys your product, he's buying you. So your personal package counts for a lot. What image do you want your company to convey? What adjectives would you use? Confident, quick and young? Or dignified, trustworthy and knowledgeable? And do you convey those impressions?

Your clothes and appearance give the buyer vital clues. They should match the buyer's clothes. Buyers like to buy from people like themselves. Dark or matt clothes convey seniority and seriousness (suitable if you are selling, for example, to solicitors or doctors), while light and shiny clothes convey youth and lightheartedness and would be appropriate to wear if you are selling to the entertainment or media world. If in doubt, dark clothes are safer. IBM used to require all its sales people to wear dark suits, white shirts and sombre ties. It wasn't by chance that the company became the biggest in the computer business.

Don't forget accessories which make statements about you. One seller in the construction business keeps a hard hat on display in his car. He doesn't often tour building sites, but it shows the architects he meets that he is in the same business.

TOUCH

If you make a grab for your would-be lover, you might frighten them off. It is vital to check for buying signals – are they ready for touch, and do they reach out to touch you?

Some cultures touch more readily, so touching the buyer will depend on the culture. Italians and French will readily kiss, while the English will not. A firm handshake is common across most cultures. A weak shake from a sweaty hand will not inspire the buyer, while a firm handshake accompanied by a firm gaze will communicate self-confidence and knowledge.

You will have to make up your own mind about extended touch gestures, including patting the buyer on the back, or clasping his hand with both of your hands.

ACTION POINTS

♥ The buyer will sum you up in the first three minutes – so make them count.

♥ Be relaxed but alert; interested but not over intense; businesslike yet friendly.

♥ Understand how buyers demonstrate their emotions through body language.

♥ If you are not getting the right signals from the buyer, take action to remedy the situation.

♥ Subtly reflecting the buyer's body language can silently show that you are in tune with his needs.

♥ Be careful about where and how you sit – the wrong posture or location can put off a buyer.

♥ Clothes send out strong signals about you and your business. Where possible match the buyer's clothes.

Seductive Words

The art of good conversation lies in getting the other person to talk about himself. This applies both in business and in love.

You get people to talk about themselves by asking questions, and in asking questions, you gain valuable information. You can use that information to win the sale, whether in your lover's heart or the buyer's order pad.

So here are the two most important things you can say to a lover or a buyer:

1. Say nothing.
2. Ask questions.

We start by looking at the value of silent listening.

BECOME AN EXPERT LISTENER

Many sales people take pride in being a good talker, a raconteur or a wit. They don't realise that the more they talk, the more boring they become.

Few people in this world are expert listeners. Active listening has the following characteristics:

- You listen to hear the buyer's feelings and needs.
- You can listen for extended periods of time, without lapses of attention.
- You give prompts, guiding the buyer towards the purchase decision.

You have two ears, two eyes, and one mouth. Use them in that proportion. Spend 40 per cent of your time listening, 40 per cent of your time watching the buyer's behaviour, and only 20 per cent of your time talking.

The value of silence

The Samaritans save hundreds of lives each year. They do it by expert listening. They are particularly skilled in saying nothing. They know that saying nothing creates a silence, making the other person feel obliged to talk. Silence is surprisingly stressful if you aren't familiar with it.

Your silence gives the buyer space to talk. It lets him say what is on his mind. Sometimes people need a space to think, or to formulate their thoughts. If you keep talking, you prevent that from happening.

At first you'll find the gaps uncomfortable. But you'll get used to them. Being at ease with the silence puts you in command of the conversation. But work out how long you want the silence to continue. Have something ready on your tongue if the buyer says nothing.

Use the forced silence sparingly. You don't want to irritate a buyer who feels you should make more effort to talk.

Prompts

How do you keep the buyer talking? One way is to use prompts. These are little words or noises which show that you are interested in what he is saying. There are words like, 'uh huh', or you can nod and say 'yes'. These prompts encourage the buyer to carry on talking.

Every so often the buyer will check to see if he is boring you. This will happen when he gets to the end of a train of thought. At this point, you should prompt him to continue.

QUESTIONS

Questioning the buyer serves to gain his attention, to show

empathy with his situation, and to learn about the organisation. It also reveals what his requirements are.

You should adopt a funnel approach in your questioning. Start with general questions, and move gradually closer to the ultimate question: 'Do you want to order?' (see Table 37).

From Table 37, you can see that specific questions about the size, quantity or price of the product do not occur until the very end of the interview. You should only ask this sort of question once you know what the client's real needs are. Such questions assume that the customer wants to buy; and you cannot establish that until you have asked many more general questions. These

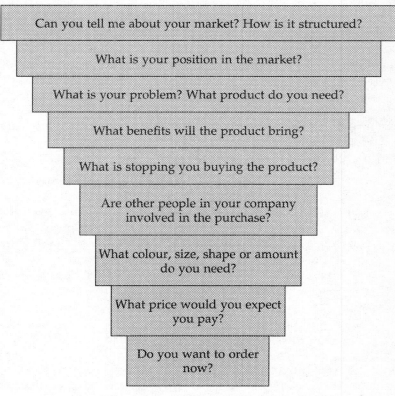

Table 37 **Funnelling of questions**

are the most revealing. They tell you what is going on inside the buyer's mind, and what motivates him. But ensure that your questions are relevant, and that they gradually become more specific, focusing more clearly all the time on the order.

Probe for the answers

Imagine you sell stair parts, and you are talking to a house builder. You might start by asking about the state of the housing market. You can narrow this down to how many houses the company plans to build this year. Next you could focus on the development in question, and ask about the style of house and the target purchaser.

Now you can probe deeper – what about the workforce's level of skill (which can vary from site to site)? Does the company have any style of stair in mind? About this point the buyer will start to sound more vague, because he won't have thought down to this level.

You can probe still further by showing him various types of stair, and asking his opinions as to their suitability. You can enquire about the type of wood, the delivery requirements, and whether there is a budget.

Two things are worth noting here:

1. You still haven't tried to 'sell' the buyer anything, even though you are probably 20 minutes into the meeting.
2. You could have simply taken away the plans and given the buyer a price based on drawings. But by asking questions, you get more information about the buyer's personal likes and dislikes. You also show your company to be thought-led and customer oriented. You've put a human face on your business, and shown yourself to be sympathetic to his problems.

What opening lines are for

In your first conversation with a potential lover, you want to seem interesting and confident, an issue we looked at in Chapter 10 from the perspective of body language. Your lover and the

Eleven chat-up lines	
Questions to ask your lover	**Questions to ask your customer**
1. Where did you live as a child? What sort of a childhood was it?	What is your role in the organisation?
2. Do you have relatives in the area?	What changes would you like to see here in five years' time?
3. Where do you live now? What sort of a place is it?	What would you like to be doing in five years' time?
4. Your job: is it interesting, challenging? Your boss?	What are the main problems you'd like to resolve right now?
5. What is the culture like at work?	What would make us effective as suppliers?
6. What do you do outside work?	What sorts of problems do your customers have?
7. Do you have any long-term plans or goals?	What problems do you find with the existing products/ services you buy?
8. What are you seeking out of life?	Who else in your organisation is involved in this decision?
9. How did you feel about (a recent political event)?	How do you regard your competitors?
10. Do you have many friends and acquaintances?	What benefit do you hope to get out of this purchase?
11. If we went out again, what would you like to do?	Do you know anyone else who needs this product?

Table 38 **Chat-up lines. Armed with a list of questions, no date will ever be traumatic again. No initial meeting with a powerful buyer will ever make you fearful**

buyer should be able to say afterwards, 'I met an interesting person who really seemed to understand me, and who was great company.'

You achieve this by asking questions. Your opening questions should be non-threatening. For example, your would-be lover would not want to reveal personal details. Some questions to ask your lover and customer are shown in Table 38.

Ask open-ended questions

Closed questions are those which can be answered with a fact, or with 'yes' or 'no'. *Open-ended questions* require a more detailed answer. So it is better to ask open questions because you get a more informative answer. Open-ended questions start with Who, What, Where, Why, When and How.

You should also avoid *leading questions*. Those are ones to which the questioner expects a particular answer. It isn't the best way to get the truth. I once heard a sales person greet a customer with the words, 'Hello, are you all right, yes?' Then he asked, 'How's business? All right?' Every question finished with an anticipated 'Yes?' These leading questions showed he wasn't going to listen to the answer.

Table 39 shows a question about a competitor, phrased in three different ways. It shows that you can get three different answers depending on the way the question is phrased.

DON'T MAKE ASSUMPTIONS

Recently I saw a sales person make a blunder. He said to a customer, 'You won't need this element – we'll take it out of our specification'. The customer opposed this, saying, 'But we saw that as a major requirement.'

The embarrassed sales person then had to agree with the customer that it *was* an important function, and that it *should* be in the specification.

This is an all-too-frequent occurrence. The sales person is too presumptuous; he thinks he knows what the client wants; and he doesn't ask the client his views. He then has to do a U-turn when

Three ways to question a buyer			
Question format	Question	Effect on the listener	Reply
Closed	Are you reasonably happy with your existing supplier?	Can only answer yes or no	Yes
Leading	Presumably you get adequate service from your existing supplier?	Is expected to answer yes	Yes, it's OK
Open	What kind of difficulties do you have with your existing supplier?	Has to reply with a full sentence	'Well, the quality is a bit variable; and we don't see much of their representative'

Table 39   **The different ways to ask a question**

the client rejects his suggestion. Asking a question is always better than making a statement. In this case, the sales person should have said, 'Is this function important to you?'

It also shows that you shouldn't rush into a sale. Take time to explore every aspect of the client's needs before making any suggestions.

GETTING THE TRUTH

The manager of our Scottish division asks clients a question, and then says disarmingly, 'You can be frank'. This simple statement produces devastatingly honest answers.

The first time I met him, he asked me what I thought of my colleagues. 'You can be frank', he reassured me. That was the first time (and hopefully the last) I ever gave a stranger unguarded opinions about other members of staff.

TALKING TO YOUR LOVER

Men and women talk differently. Male talk tends to be more direct, more action-oriented. Female talk tends to be more connected to the emotions. That is why the two genders often fail to communicate properly. So the next time your lover seems to be talking strangely, reflect that it may simply be a gender difference.

Try to communicate in ways that your lover will understand. And encourage your lover to understand your moods and needs. One woman, who had split from her husband, said that the best thing about the divorce was no longer having to talk about football.

Talking to your lover

- *Say the words*: Some lovers (especially men) find it difficult to say, 'I love you'. Once you get used to it, it gets easier. You may even get to like it. So practise the words. Demonstrate your affection.
- *Keep it simple*: You don't have to sound like a Victorian poet. Just saying 'I love you' is enough. And it's better to say: 'I love you more than anything in this world' than to say: 'I think you are the most heavenly, beautiful, adorable and exquisite human being in all the world'.
- *Keep it sincere*: Your lover will detect insincerity. Find out what you particularly admire about your lover, and communicate it.
- *Say it often*: Your lover needs regular reassurance. Tell your lover at every possible opportunity, 'I love you.'
- *Say it when it is unexpected*: If you only say 'I love you' when you part in the morning, it becomes a cliché. Express your love at unexpected times.
  If you only take your lover out on anniversaries or birthdays, you lose spontaneity. Demonstrate affection when you don't need to.

Table 40   **How to use the language of love. Tell your customers you need them, too**

COMPLIMENTS

The lover: Lovers bask in compliments, so give them freely – but ensure they are subtle and genuine. Emphasise only the points that are credible. Use a compliment to frame a question which will allow the lover to talk at length. For example: 'Your hair has been nicely styled; where do you have it done?'

The buyer: Compliment the size of his organisation, its success, its growth, or its management. Buyers are as vain as anyone else; and even the most jaded of buyers wants to believe in the excellence of his business.

DON'T TALK ABOUT YOURSELF

The buyer is not interested in you. I repeat: you are not of interest to the buyer. He is only interested in:

1. how you can help him personally; and
2. how you can help his business.

This means you should not talk about yourself. The only exception is to give information which:

1. tells him you understand his needs ('I worked on a similar project for XYZ Co.);
2. makes you seem similar to him ('Yes, I saw that match, too');
3. reveals a personal detail which illustrates your humanity or need for support ('I have that problem, too').

Don't seek to crown his stories. If he says his firm has ten buyers, don't tell him you've just come from a company which has 20 buyers.

USE THE WORD 'YOU'

A good lover will frequently use the word 'You'. A selfish lover will spend his time using the word 'I'.

It is easy to keep using the word 'we' when talking to a

customer. You use this word every time you talk about your product or your business. The more you say 'You', the more you are focusing on the client's needs. The more you say 'We', the more you are thinking about yourself.

DELAY YOUR PRODUCT STORY

Do not talk about your company or product for the first third of the meeting, especially if the buyer's requirement is complex. Unless, that is, the buyer asks you about it. If you get three-quarters of the way through your normal interview time, and the buyer has not asked about your product, he isn't interested in buying.

If you avoid talking about your product, you can gauge the extent of the customer's interest in buying, because any mention of the product will be initiated by him. It's like being a firefighter. You're in the fire station actively waiting for the alarm to go off.

You should be seeking information, meanwhile, about the market and the buyer's role in the market. If you sell cat food, you can be asking the buyer about his stores, about cat food and cat owners, without necessarily talking about your brand. Sometimes I wait until the customer says, 'But enough about me. Tell me about your service.' Then I know he is ready to listen.

ASK THE CLIENT'S HELP

Respect the client's knowledge and experience. Ask his support in putting your package together. Say to him:

- If you were me, what would you include in the package?
- In your experience, what do your managers find most persuasive?
- Where in the plant would you want the hoists?

Customers are pleased to be asked. You are paying them a compliment, and allowing them to air their knowledge. It also helps you unlock their needs. When the customer says, 'I would start with the manual staff', you save yourself the embarrassment of starting a sales pitch with the words, 'We normally start with the senior engineers'.

SELL BENEFITS NOT FEATURES

Features are aspects of the product's performance. Designers, production and R&D people like quoting features, because they are factual, and they can be tested.

Customers don't buy features; they buy benefits. Benefits are what the features mean to the customer.

Some features and benefits for a new car are shown in Table 41. The features are translated into benefits by adding the words 'which means that'.

Does your company sell features or benefits?

Go through your sales literature. Highlight all the words which are *features*. Then mark in a different colour all the words which are *benefits*.

What is the ratio of features to benefits? Benefits should be at least as numerous as the features, and ideally they should out-

Features and benefits of a car		
Feature	*which means ...*	Benefit
0–60mph in 8 seconds		Fast acceleration at traffic lights
50mpg		Motoring is cheaper
Lifetime warranty on parts		No worries about maintenance costs
4 models and 10 colours		More individual motoring
Sun roof		Fresh air on sunny days

Table 41 **Selling benefits**

number the features. Your leaflet probably has more features than benefits. Is the same true of your sales presentation?

Benefits should be quantified. Always give a figure. *How much* extra profit? *What percentage* increase?

SELL PROBLEMS AND SOLUTIONS

Firms in the computer industry are sometimes accused of 'box shifting'. This means selling computers in cardboard boxes without trying to understand why the customer needs them. It is something we all do sometimes, no matter what the product. That is why it is useful to look at problems and solutions. Table 42 show problems and solutions from three different markets.

This is important because until you have established what the customer's problem is, you can't define a solution. And if you can't define the solution, you can't define what package to offer your customer. Worse still, you might formulate your product offering to solve the *wrong* problem. For example, the wrong solutions to the three problems below would be:

1. Our computer system is ideal for use in a network.
2. Our fleet management services will save you lots of money.
3. We can offer a choice of tarmacadam or concrete road surfaces.

You can define the right problem by asking the customer, 'What is your single biggest problem?' Remember, if your customer

Your problem	Our solution
1. Your accounts are in a mess	Our computer system will organise your accounts
2. Your car fleet is an administrative burden	Our fleet management services will make life easy for you
3. You need this bridge built on time	We will guarantee to complete the bridge on time

Table 42 **Defining problems and solutions**

does not think he has a problem, he won't see any reason to change. That means he won't buy your product. So it is vital to identify the customer's problem, and to ensure that he knows he has a problem.

SELLING THE FUTURE

You can extend the Problem-Solution strategy by taking the customer into the future, and showing him the wisdom of his purchase.

Tell the customer: 'Your machines will be more reliable. They'll break down less often. The workforce will be happier. And your maintenance costs will be reduced. All because you opted for the Reliability Centred Maintenance programme. In a year's time, your life will be simpler'.

You can do the same thing with your lover. If you want to go out, and you lover wants to stay in, you could say, 'Your friends are probably sitting there, and the music is playing, and everyone is having fun. The band is about to go on stage, and they are selling those new cocktails you like'.

DISTRACTIONS

There are plenty of buyers who welcome the arrival of a sales person, particularly if they have useful information, or if they sell interesting products.

The three things you should tell a customer

P-E International, a management consultancy, tells its consultants: In your sales pitch and in your written proposal, tell the client only three things:

1. Why he should *buy*.
2. Why he should buy *from us*.
3. Why he should buy *now*.

These distractions can work in your favour if you're seeking to establish a rapport with the customer. But beware of spending an hour with the customer, to find later that you only discussed fishing. Keep in mind the real purpose of your visit – to sell him your product.

WORD OF MOUTH

Most people meet their lover through a social network. Many purchase decisions are made in the same way. Companies devalue the importance of these networks. They prefer to reach out to the customer by advertising. But according to research, social networks play a major role in influencing purchases. So bear in mind that your aunt Josie might be a valuable sales person.

This happens especially in markets like financial services. 'Information is often sought from friends or relatives working in the financial services sector,' says one research report, 'when people are seeking these products'. This means you should socialise as much as possible.

HARNESS THE POWER OF ENDORSEMENT

When you say your product is great, the customer won't fully believe you. He knows you want the sale. You need an independent person to say the words for you. Endorsement is a powerful tool. There are two steps you can take:

1. Ask existing customers why they buy from you. Is it product quality, customer service or reliability? Ask them if you can use their comments. Then type up their comments and show them to prospects.

2. Ask a customer if you can give prospects his telephone number. Armed with the names of satisfied customers, you can say to a prospect, 'Ring up this person. He bought our product. He can tell you what he thinks of it.'

ACTION POINTS

♥ Become an expert listener. Use prompts to encourage the buyer to continue.

♥ Use open-ended questions to get fuller answers. Probe to maximise your understanding of a problem.

♥ Don't rush into a sale; and don't make assumptions about what a customer wants.

♥ Give compliments freely but honestly.

♥ Don't talk about yourself. The customer doesn't want to hear about you, except what you can do for him.

♥ Delay telling your product story until the customer is weary of the sound of his own voice.

♥ Define the features and benefits of your product or service.

♥ Sell problems and solutions.

♥ Sell the future; tell the buyer how your product will make his life better.

♥ Use customer testimonials to clinch a sale.

Overcoming Resistance

Buyers often resist the charms of sales people, just as lovers resist the wooing of a suitor. There are many reasons: the timing may be wrong; the buyer may have no need for the product; or the lover may find the suitor unattractive. All these things are reasonable and predictable.

But sales people are often taught to bully the buyer into giving an order. They are expected to treat the buyer as an enemy, someone to overcome. This approach no longer works. Most buyers want a long-term relationship based on mutual advantage and honesty. Woolworth, with its 800 stores in the UK, says to visiting suppliers, 'Here is our plan for your products for the next three years. Now tell us how we fit into *your* plans.'

You should treat the customer as a friend to be helped. If he truly doesn't want your product, there is no point in trying to trick him into buying it. A buyer's objections can be the sign of a poor or new relationship. They show that the buyer doesn't know you. They show that he feels unwanted. Why should he give you an order within an hour of meeting you for the first time?

Objections may also show that the buyer has other suitors who give better service.

So the art of seductive selling is to look after your customer so well as to prevent objections. In a well managed relationship, the buyer and seller should be able to discuss problems with a view to resolving them, not as a defensive mechanism.

OVERCOMING RESISTANCE TO SEX

Of course, objections and rejection don't take place just in the customer's office. They also occur in the back row of the cinema or at the end of a date. So we start by looking at objections to sex.

Faced with a lover who says 'I'm not ready for sex,' what should you do? Can you overcome this objection?

Ideally, you shouldn't allow that situation to arise. If a lover says no, it means that you have misread the signals, and blundered into a rejection. Read the chapter on body language before making any more sexual advances.

The ideal situation is to have a lover crawling after you on hands and knees begging you for sex – that rarely happens to any of us! But we can achieve the next best thing, which is to create a situation where the lover actively wants sex.

In the case of an objection, you should identify the reasons for your lover's reticence, and overcome them, before you 'ask for the order' by making a pass. Once you've allowed a lover to reject your offer, you'll find it very difficult to alter that decision. Simply saying the word 'no' creates a break. A lover who has said no is feeling self-assertive.

Finding out a would-be lover's real objections aren't easy. Most of us would never dream of saying to someone's face: 'You're boring and you've got spots'. As in the sales process, you should ask your lover questions:

- Why don't you want to make love?
- How would you want me to change?
- How do you feel about love?

If your would-be lover has a best friend or confidant, maybe that person will tell you about your chances of success. Or ask the office gossip – some people know everything that's going on.

WHY DID YOU FAIL?

In love, objections fall into two categories:

1. *Objections that centre on you or your lover.* Is the problem about you (for example, your manner)? Or is it a problem that affects your partner (for example, being in love with someone else, or being scared of involvement)?
2. *Objections which can be changed, and those which cannot.* Some objections are fundamental (like your height). Others can be overcome (like an accent, bad breath or a sexist attitude).

Now fill in Table 43. Identify the objections which are preventing you from consummating your relationship.

Try to distinguish between the *real* problem, and what the Samaritans call the *'presenting* problem' (one which is convenient to mention). Your would-be lover may offer a plausible comment (for example, 'I'm too busy to have a serious relationship'), when the real problem may be something completely different.

By now you should have identified the objections. Next you should decide how to overcome them. Filling in Table 44 will help you do this. Try to suggest a solution for every problem you have identified.

If you have one or more objections which can't be overcome, maybe you need to consider looking for another lover? If so, it's back to Chapter 1, to start all over again!

How to identify the reasons for resistance to love		
	You	Your partner
Things that can be changed		
Things that can't be changed		

Table 43 **Fill in here any reasons for reticence about love which your lover might have**

Objection	Solution

Table 44 **How to overcome resistance to love**

SALES OBJECTIONS

It is better to forestall objections than counter them. When a customer makes an objection, it shows that you haven't prepared him properly. You haven't given him all the information he needs.

In a sales presentation, you can't forestall every objection that a customer could possibly mention – that would take hours. But in your assessment of the customer's needs you should anticipate what objections each client is likely to voice. You can say, 'Now some people might say we're expensive, but...'. Or you might say, 'You can buy this sort of product in fibreglass, but...'. In doing this, you expose the customer's concerns to debate, and you reassure him with your answers to them.

Which objections really count?

Not every objection raised by a customer really counts. A customer may be willing to accept one or more disadvantages if he thinks that your product is the best overall.

I recently went to test drive a car. I complained to the salesman that the foot pedals were too close together. The salesman admitted that they were closer than on my existing car. Sensibly, he said no more about it. I had already decided that the car I was testing was the best overall choice for my needs.

If you try to overcome a customer's every objection, you'll end up sounding too clever. Sometimes customers like to voice objections to stay in control of the conversation, to show that they aren't desperate for your product, or to voice technical knowledge.

Being a buyer can be stressful, because the salesperson usually knows more about the product than the customer. So if the customer taps the keyboard keys unfavourably, or casts doubts on the colour, he may only be trying to assert himself.

Probe to find how important the objection is. Ask the customer, 'Would that stop you buying?'

Is it a 'must have' objection?

Imagine a buyer who objects that your gadget hasn't got variable speeds. Is that a 'must have' or a 'nice to have'? You will have to treat each of these two situations differently.

- *Handling a 'nice to have' objection*: Agree with the buyer that the feature would indeed be nice to have. Tell him you'll mention his comment to your firm.
- *Handling a 'must have' objection*: Can you incorporate the requirement at an extra cost? Can you persuade the buyer that it is really a 'nice to have' attribute? If so, your product benefits may outweigh this drawback.

  If you can't convince the buyer to change a 'must have' into a 'nice to have', you may have to change your product specification if you want the sale.

The price

Pricing is like desire. The more desirable a buyer finds your product or service, the more he will be prepared to pay for it. Similarly, the more a lover wants you, the more they will do for you. There are several steps in attraction, as Table 45 shows.

Your price reflects your negotiating power. The stronger your brand image, the higher your price will be. Market leaders are

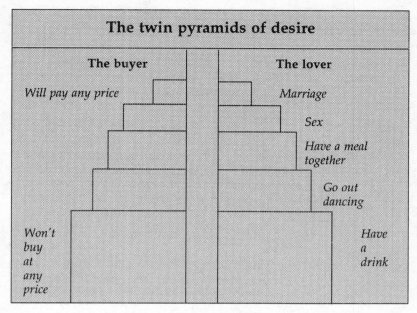

The twin pyramids of desire

The buyer	The lover
Will pay any price	Marriage
	Sex
	Have a meal together
	Go out dancing
Won't buy at any price	Have a drink

Table 45 **How far up the two pyramids are you?**

usually price leaders. They have the highest prices, and they are usually the first to raise them.

Remember, too, that the better the service, the more the buyer will come to rely on you. Then you will find it easier to gain a higher price.

Someone, somewhere will always be cheaper than you

Someone will always offer your buyer a cheaper price than you can. So you have to get used to selling against price. If the buyer suggests that he can buy your product more cheaply elsewhere, don't panic.

Table 46 shows eight ways to counter price resistance.

Avoid the word 'cheap' (unless agreeing that 'some of our competitors offer cheap goods'). It is best to talk about 'value for

Eight ways to counter price resistance

1. *Emphasise value*	Remind the buyer that a competitor's product might be cheaper, but if it falls apart, doesn't do the job it's supposed to do, or if it operates slowly, the buyer will face a continuing problem. At the least this will be an irritation. At worst, it will be an additional hidden cost.
2. *Compare in scale*	Tell the customer how small the cost is compared with his overall budget. Say, 'At £10 000 the alarm system is just 5% of the total cost of the new warehouse. Think, too, of the cost of re-building the warehouse after a fire. Imagine the cost of lost stock and annoyed customers. These would greatly outweigh the cost of the alarm.'
3. *Offer a modular package*	You can pre-empt price competition by dividing your product into different elements. This allows the customer to buy only those parts which he needs. An engineering business might separate development, prototype production, mass production, installation, servicing and maintenance. This frees the purchaser from commiting himself to a large financial outlay.
4. *Avoid direct comparison*	You can also make it difficult to compare the price by offering a different pack size, a different formula, or a different range of features. Call the product by a different name.
5. *Offer a price pledge*	A price pledge (offering to match any competitor's price) allows you to win work when you are the preferred supplier but a competitor offers a lower price. You may have to undertake work at low prices. But you wouldn't make a price-matching guarantee unless you were anxious to get work.

Table 46 **Overcoming price resistance**

Eight ways to counter price resistance (Cont.)

6. *Offer the minimum*	If you know that a company will go to tender, and will accept the lowest tender, offer the client a cut-down, no-frills product. As the job progresses, identify work that is outside the scope of the contract, and ask for more money. If the client is happy with the job, he will usually agree.
7. *Offer a finance package*	Instead of selling it to the customer, you could rent it, lease it, or offer credit terms. This reduces the scale and permanence of the buying decision, which makes the purchase commitment easier.
8. *Identify savings*	Demonstrate in writing the savings that your product will bring. A sample chart is shown in Table 47

Table 46 **Overcoming price resistance**

money' or 'less expensive'. To the buyer, 'cheap' may mean poor quality.

HOW TO OVERCOME SIX COMMON OBJECTIONS

1. The delay objection: 'I'll need to think about it'

This often conceals a more fundamental objection which the buyer doesn't want to reveal, so it is important to probe for the buyer's real concerns.

Counter with: 'What aspects of the product do you need to think about?'

The buyer may decide to come clean, and tell you: he really wants to get other quotes.

A variant of the delay objection is, 'I'll need to get clearance from my boss'. If this is genuine (he really can't buy), kick yourself for wasting time talking to someone without the authority to buy. However, he may genuinely want to achieve consensus among his colleagues on the purchase. If this is the

Savings opportunities chart	
Benefits of our product	**Savings you will achieve (£)**
Longer life	
Greater efficiency	
Less depreciation	
Reduction in down time	
Long-term savings	
Less frequent repairs	
Reduction in management time	
(Other)	
Total	

Table 47 **Customise this table to suit your product. Then fill out this table with your buyer's help. It will show him the reasons for buying your product, and will also give him valuable information to persuade the board in your favour**

case, kick yourself again for not establishing who else needed to be involved in the conversation.

Counter with: 'Let's have a joint meeting with your boss/relevant colleagues.'

Some sales people ask the buyer, 'If I was able to overcome all your objections, would you buy?' If the buyer agrees, the way is clear to find out all the buyer's objections.

2. Overstocked objection: 'I've still got your last order on the shelves'.

You can see for yourself whether this is true or not. If it is true, you should see how you can help him increase his sales, perhaps through sales promotion or co-operative advertising.

3. Competitor loyalty objection: 'We normally buy from X. They give us excellent prices and service'.

Say to the buyer: 'Do you know about the benefits from buying from a supplier like us?' Then list the advantages.

Or say to him, 'It's worth having two suppliers. That way you can compare one against the other. It will also keep your main supplier from becoming complacent.'

4. Competitor performance objection: 'We buy from X because we and they have a computer-linked ordering system'.

Say to the buyer, 'Tell us your specification, and we'll install one, too.'

5. Buying requirement objection: 'You haven't got ISO 9000'.

This objection relates to a failing in your product or service. First probe how serious the objection is. If you can remedy the problem, use counter 1. If you can't remedy it, use counters 2 or 3:

- *Counter 1 (We conform to your requirement)*: 'We're in the process of applying for it. Come and audit our plant, and see our quality.'
- *Counter 2 (Convert it to a 'nice to have')*: Convince him that this isn't an important issue. 'Surely it's more important to get the right product than a piece of paper?'
- *Counter 3 (The exception)*: See if the company has ever made an exception. Ask, 'Has an exception ever been made?' The customer will often say, 'Yes, we once needed some cleanser, and ...'. Because the buyer narrates the story, he begins to own the idea of 'making an exception'. If you had merely said, 'Can't you make an exception, just this once' he would be likely to say 'no'.

6. Ordering ban objection: 'We have a ban on ordering'.

Counter this objection with: 'If you don't buy, you won't be able to make your product'. Or, 'You'll be out of stock; you'll lose sales; and you'll upset your customers'.

How do you overcome objections?	
Objection	Solution
1.	
2.	
3.	
4.	
5.	
6.	

Table 48   **Write down the objections your buyers put forward. Then show how you counter them**

CREATING A SENSE OF URGENCY

My colleague Jim was trying to sell a client a set of conferences. At the end of his presentation, he said, 'Your competitors are beginning to organise this sort of event. If you want to run the conferences, you ought to do it now. If you leave it too late, you'll lose the initiative. You won't be the first. And we aren't going to meet again for several weeks, which is another reason for getting agreement today.'

The client bit his lip, and said, 'Yes, and my boss isn't going to thank me if we don't get this show on the road'. With that he gave the go-ahead.

One of the best ways of overcoming delaying objections is by instilling a sense of urgency. Tell the client what he'll miss if he doesn't order.

MAKE SURE THE CLIENT HEARS YOU

The client won't always hear you counter his objection. He may not be listening to your comment. Some people don't listen to what others have to say. So watch the client's reaction to your words. Has he really heard what you said? Keep probing to see whether any of his objections are still unresolved.

MAKE SURE THE CLIENT AGREES WITH YOU

If the client says, 'Yes, but . . .' you'll know that he has heard what you said, but not accepted your point of view.

The words 'Yes, but . . .' signal an objection. Listen hard to what the client says. Is he re-stating the current objection, perhaps from a different perspective ('Yes, but my Finance Director will still think it's too much')? If so, you'll have to look at the problem from that angle ('OK, let's see if we can produce a no-frills specification which meets that concern').

Alternatively, he may be moving to a new objection. ('Yes, the price is all right, *but* I'm not sure the pump is powerful enough'.)

NEGOTIATION

Lovers have always sparred. Until the act of love takes place, neither partner knows whether or not the sparring will end with love making.

Every male suspects that an initial rejection doesn't stop a woman from saying 'yes' on the next date. And many a girl suspects that her boyfriend still loves her even if he ignores her because he is watching football on television.

Lots of buyers negotiate with sales people. They try to get extra value for money. Often they find the supplier they want, and then they try to squeeze some extra benefit out of the deal. Some buyers do this out of habit; others do it because they need to show off to their boss.

Start by assessing the relative strength of the buyer and yourself. The more the buyer needs you, the less you have to concede. If, after a tender process, the buyer has decided to buy from you, you don't need to concede. Likewise, it's important to watch the buyer's body language. If he reveals buying signals, you have less need to concede.

Decide why the buyer is pushing for a better deal. What does he want to get out of it? Sometimes a buyer will be happy with any sort of concession, no matter how minor, because he feels inadequate without one.

Work out what losing the deal will cost you. You stand to suffer a lot more by losing one of your biggest customers than you do a small one.

RESPONDING TO THE BUYER'S DEMAND

The buyer usually seeks to get more product for the same money. You can respond to this with a counter offer. For example, you could agree to a buyer's demand for a discount, providing:

- you can deliver the goods to one central warehouse instead of ten depots;
- you can reduce the quality from Top Grade to Medium Grade;
- he can accept one drop per month instead of weekly deliveries;
- he can second two of his people to help with the extra paperwork.

If the buyer changes course, and seeks a different extra benefit, you can match his tactics by suggesting yet another response. 'Yes, we can deliver the goods Free on Board rather than just to the docks, providing you can place an order for three months supply now.' Or you may send him a revised tender showing the discount he asked for, but with a matching extra cost somewhere else in the document.

Building in a concession

Sometimes it is wise to build a spare margin into the price. Then, if the buyer asks for a 10 per cent reduction, you can 'grudgingly' give it.

Conceding for the first order only

If you have to give a concession, make sure your paperwork shows that this is only for a special order or an initial period of time. Show the order as a 'Special introductory offer'. Once the buyer commits himself by buying from you, he loses some of his bargaining power. When he wants to repeat the order, put the price back to the original figure.

Psyching out the buyer

Emotional blackmail is a powerful tool which can disarm the strongest executive. It is also justified against a buyer who casually and automatically demands discounts.

Potential rape victims have sometimes escaped harm by telling the attacker about themselves. Similarly, the buyer can't get aggressive towards you if he knows you have a dog named Humphrey, that you hope to get the job of Sales Manager, and that the telesales girl is going on holiday to Vancouver. A good way to psyche out a buyer is to get close to him. If he plays tennis with you, and you visit his home at Christmas, how can he later demand discounts from you?

You can also make him feel part of your team. Invite his views. Get him along to your social events. If a buyer demands discounts, appeal to his self-interest and sense of fair play. Say to him, 'We have to pitch our price at a rate that pays our costs and allows for investment. It's in your interest to let us achieve that. We need to stay in business. Already suppliers are going out of business. If we went out of business, you could end up with fewer, more powerful suppliers'.

You can also make him feel guilty. 'If I give away this kind of discount, I'm going to have to lay off people.' You can even hand him your internal phone list, and say, 'Which of these people do you want to fire?'

ACTION POINTS

♥ Be aware of the objections a customer could make, and forestall them.

♥ Don't counter every objection – let the buyer win a few points. Decide which are the *real* objections. Give concessions.

♥ Design a savings chart, and ask the buyer to help you fill in the numbers.

♥ Create a sense of urgency – tell the buyer what he may lose.

♥ When countering objections, make sure the buyer hears you, and agrees with you.

♥ Listen for the words, 'Yes, but . . .', and look for the objection that is hidden there.

♥ Counter a buyer's demand for extra value with a matching requirement ('We'll accept X if you'll accept Y').

♥ Get so close to the buyer he can't turn you down.

Climax

Closing In

There comes a time in every relationship when you have to make a request. You have to ask for a date. You have to ask for a more physical relationship. Or you have to ask, 'Will you marry me?'

These are the most difficult questions to ask. To a few people, they come easily. The rest of us have to screw up our courage, for by asking these questions, we expose ourselves to rejection.

The same applies in selling. The best sales people enjoy the thrill of the sell. They can take rejection. But we all have to ask for the order, even if it makes us anxious.

There are ways of minimising this anxiety and reducing the chance of rejection. You can check the buyer's body language, which we discussed in Chapter 10, and in 'Six Buying Signals' in Table 49. You can also 'qualify' your sales lead by asking a series of questions, which will tell you whether he is ready to buy. These are discussed under 'Trial Close' below. But at the end of the day, you have to ask the buyer, 'Do you want it?'

THE BUYER MUST BE A WILLING PARTNER

Sales people have been taught various methods of getting the customer to buy. Any close which involves sales tricks may work for inexpensive purchases but not for complex big ticket items.

You can trick a customer into buying a product, but the repercussions will cause you problems. They include:

- cancelling the order in the days following your visit;
- rejecting the product after it arrives because it wasn't really wanted;
- refusal to pay the invoice;
- using the product, finding it isn't suitable, and never buying from you again.

In the same way, you might get a lover to sleep with you once as a result of too much alcohol. But the morning after is likely to be sour, and you won't gain a long-term relationship.

NEVER FORCE YOUR LOVER

Force can never be used against a lover: no long-term relationship was ever built on brutality. Likewise, you can't force a customer to buy your product. If a customer decides that he doesn't like the product, no amount of foot-in-the-door tactics will make him change his mind.

In one of Aesop's fables, the wind and the sun had a bet to see who could take off a traveller's cloak. The wind blew vigorously. But the harder he blew, the more the traveller wrapped his cloak about himself.

Then the sun took over. He shone gently at first, and then gradually grew warmer. As the traveller walked along the road, he began to sweat, and it wasn't long before he removed his cloak. It just shows that understanding a customer's needs is the best way to get results.

WATCH FOR THE BUYING SIGNALS

The buyer frowns and starts to discuss the price of your goods. Don't panic. This is an excellent signal. Talking money is the clearest possible buying signal. In his mind, he has moved beyond asking himself *whether* he should buy, to ask '*How* can I pay for it?'

In Table 49 are six buying signals which tell you when a customer is ready to buy.

Six buying signals
1. The buyer asks about your product or company
2. The buyer talks about a problem he needs to solve.
3. The buyer displays non-verbal buying signals (see 'Use your body').
4. The buyer starts modifying details in your proposal ('we wouldn't want the security marking ... the network would need to include our R&D department').
5. The buyer starts talking about the cost of the product.
6. The buyer asks 'Where do we go from here?' or 'what's the next step?'

Table 49 **Buying signals**

DIFFERENT TYPES OF CLOSE

The alternative close

Here you give the customer two options for purchase ('Would you like us to deliver on Monday or Thursday?'). It's like saying to your lover, 'Your place or mine?'. This type of close will not work if the customer is not ready to buy.

The presumptive close

Here you assume that the customer wants to buy, and so you ask, 'So you'll want six cases of our regular size, then?' It's like unbuttoning your lover's clothing without asking approval. Presumption is not the most pleasant of traits; it is closely linked to arrogance and selfishness.

Trial close

The trial close is what a lover might prefer. It is used when you suspect that a lover is ready for love, or a customer is ready to buy.

On a date, you can hold your lover's hand, put your arm

around your lover's waist, or whisper in your lover's ear. Your lover's response will tell you whether to go further, or to stop.

With a buyer, the trial close will involve asking tentative questions:

- 'How do you feel about our products?'
- 'Are you likely to start stocking this kind of range?'
- 'If we were able to provide the kind of services you're looking for, would you use us?'

The response from the buyer will let you decide whether to ask for the order.

ASKING FOR THE ORDER

In the old days, 'the order' was usually something tangible, like an insurance policy or a two dozen assorted pencils. Today, the order is just as likely to be the buyer's agreement to:

- maintain the same level of 'facings' in the store, or to continue to stock your brand;
- put you on the tender list;
- present your proposals to the Board;
- fix a further meeting with the buyer's colleagues;
- evaluate a trial quantity of your product.

In few of these cases are we asking the buyer to give us an order. Often the sales process is spread over weeks or even years. Often the customer's agreement is never gained in the sales interview. It may come in a fax or a letter, several weeks after the final presentation, and after the customer has evaluated several competing bids.

In some cultures, moving to a sale is painfully slow. In Japan, I got agreement from four Unilever executives that they needed our sort of services. For over an hour, they all agreed that they had pressing problems. Sensing victory, I told them I would send a free proposal indicating our plan of action and outlining some costs. There was uproar. The executives said they had no power to ask for a proposal. They would have to consult with other colleagues. This couldn't be rushed. Like other Westerners before me, I left the meeting mystified.

But you should always try to achieve your objective at each meeting. Many sales people avoid asking for the order. They chat to the customer, assume he doesn't want to buy anything, and leave. They are not doing the job they are paid for.

In any meeting with a customer, you should be looking for ways in which he can buy your product or use more of it. That is your skill. Anyone can chat to customers – only you can sell.

Create a win-win situation

For the customer to buy, you need a win-win situation. You get the order, so your win is clear to see.

But how does the buyer win? He has to get something out of the purchase. The deal has to solve a problem or make him feel good. This means that before a customer will buy, you have to identify and communicate what he is going to get out of the deal.

Keep asking until you get a firm answer

Once you get to the threshold of a sale – with a lover or a customer – never yield until you get a firm 'yes' or 'no'. Many sales have foundered because the sales person gave up. Many relationships have succeeded because the lover was persistent. Sometimes the person you want acquiesces because your attention is flattering. People want to feel needed. They will bestow their affection – and their orders – on the person who needs them.

If you write a proposal or a tender, you should follow it up with a phone call asking, 'Did you get it?'. You should do this even if you send it by courier. It gives you a reason to call the prospect, and to judge his reaction to it. It allows you to see whether the customer wants to alter the specification. You can also see how your price compares with the competition. If the client can't give an instant answer, you should ask if you can ring in a few weeks' time. Serious buyers respect this approach. You may have to track clients over 18 months before landing an order. If you present tenders or proposals, an enquiry tracking system is essential.

Often a company will decide that it doesn't want the product for which it invited tenders. But the company may need something else. So don't assume that if he doesn't respond to your tender he doesn't want to place an order. It may simply be that the specification has changed. **So even if the buyer doesn't buy, you should ask, 'Is there anything else you need, either now or in the near future?'**

The buyer may be desperate for it, too

The buyer may want to buy just as much as you want to sell. He may be under pressure to complete the project on time, and your product may be essential in helping him do that. So don't assume that every sales meeting will be uphill; nor should you assume that every buyer is hostile.

When it comes to love, your partner may also be keen to consummate the relationship. Your partner may see you as a desirable lover. He or she may not have had a deep relationship for a long time. So, like selling, the pursuit of love is sometimes easier than you would think.

Trial start

A trial marriage is one way of seeing how compatible you are. It allows two people to live together without too much commitment. The same applies in selling. Customers like being able to try a product without too much commitment.

Getting a small, trial-size pack means not having to make a major financial commitment to an unknown brand. The trial size is priced cheaply to encourage the non-user to buy it. The pack is too small to encourage existing users to switch from full-price normal sized packs, so the price cut won't affect your normal revenue. Its small size adds novelty to an otherwise predictable shopping trip. The customer feels as though he is giving himself a present.

Trial is quite feasible in other markets. Photocopier companies leave a machine at a prospect's office on free loan for a month. The client gets so used to the machine that he wants to keep it.

Public relations consultancies undertake a free pitch for a prospective client. They hope that the company will be so impressed with their creative ideas that the client will appoint them to do his PR.

In short, if you can give the customer a small sample of your product, you should do so. It makes it easy for the customer to change his buying behaviour.

Starting small

Size isn't important, in terms of the first order. It is the sale itself that counts. A trusted supplier is often asked to do extra work, so it can be worth seeking a small order because you may be given extra orders once you start.

Lovers, too, often start with small acts of stroking. Later these can lead to petting and eventually to lovemaking. Each successful physical contact can lead lovers to greater intimacy. It takes time for lovers to get to know each other, and the same appplies to buyers.

Handling rejection

You've asked for a date, or an order, and you've been turned down. Whether you're looking for love or a sale, the feelings are the same. You are going to feel hurt.

Find out why you lost. Ask whether your friend has someone else in mind. Ask the buyer why he gave the order to another company. Was it the price, or was it some other factor? When you've got the answer, see if you need to alter your strategy. Do you need to go for a different sort of lover? Do you need to dress more smartly? Do you need to anticipate and overcome a specific objection?

When all else fails ...

Be ready to make the customer an offer he can't refuse. Here are three such offers.

1. Let us give you a quotation. You'll see that our product and price is second to none.
2. Let us give you a trial amount. Only by using it can you see how good it is.

3. Let us give you some on approval. If you don't like it, return it within 30 days, and you'll owe us nothing.

You may also get a sale by offering an unrepeatable bargain, such as a reduction for a first order.

Salvage another name

There are some magic words you can use at the end of any interview. They are particularly useful at the end of an unsuccessful meeting. The words are, 'Do you know anyone else who might want my product?'

This works well in organisations where there are many buyers. A large architect's practice could have 30 architects, and if the one you visit doesn't need your sanitary ware, he may know another who does.

Similarly, a buyer may attend meetings of local business organisations, or trade association meetings, or he may have moved from another company recently. If he suggests a company to visit, you should also ask for a contact name. You then have the perfect entrée to this prospect. You can ring and say 'Mr Jones at Global Fixings suggested I give you a call'. If you have no success at this call, you know what to say at the end of the conversation: salvage another name.

You can salvage another name in love, too. You may recognise by your partner's evasions or objections that you aren't getting anywhere. If that happens, you can turn the conversation to other people who might need a lover. Your partner is likely to know someone who wants love.

ACTION POINTS

♥ Don't try to force or trick a buyer into a sale. This will rebound to your disadvantage.

♥ Watch for buying signals. Don't ask for an order until you spot them.

♥ A trial close will give you useful information about the buyer's state of mind.

♥ You should seek to get a result at every meeting.

♥ Once you have met a buyer and offered him your product, insist on a 'yes' or 'no' answer. Keep after him no matter how long it takes.

♥ Trial size orders allow the buyer to sample your product without making a big commitment. The size of the first order is not important.

♥ Be prepared to make the buyer an offer he can't refuse.

♥ Salvage another buyer's name, especially in a meeting where the customer doesn't buy.

Continue The
Relationship

14

Keeping It Up

There are two types of lover – the one you're with, and the one that you'd *like* to be with. We often ignore our own lover, and dream about the people we can't get.

The same is true of customers. We often ignore our existing customers or take them for granted. Sales people are always looking for the next order, quite forgetting the customer who is paying today's bills. The best source of new business is your existing customer. It is he who is more likely to give you more business. And it costs five times as much to recruit a new customer as to service an existing one, so keeping existing customers makes financial sense. Moreover, you can sell an existing customer other products from your range, and you can get him to upgrade to more expensive products. With a new customer, you have to start from nothing.

I visited a egg firm on behalf of my company. The manager told me, 'We haven't seen anyone from your company since it helped us install our new system, and that was 18 months ago.' I discovered that in ignoring this customer we had missed big sales opportunities. Once the system was installed we lost interest in the customer. Yet the customer had developed and expanded the system, and we had lost business.

Looking after your existing customers is also important emotionally. Every sales person has a stressful life, constantly facing the threat of rejection from customers. Having a group of loyal customers reduces the stress, and gives you a feeling of true worth.

The same applies to the relationship with your lover. Having a stable love life, and knowing that you are appreciated by your lover, is vital.

LIFETIME VALUE

Talking of worth, your lover probably does more for you than you think. Your lover puts up with your bad moods, your failure to say thank you, and your flirtations. If you added up all the things your lover does for you over a five year period, you might be surprised. Picture the piles of washing, and the evenings waiting for you because you were out with your friends.

Your customer is in the same situation. Picture not just the small order that he places each month, but the total amount he buys over a five year period. Add up the total value of his five years' purchasing. All of a sudden, the small order becomes worth thousands of pounds.

This concept, called **Lifetime Value**, also takes into account all the extra business you can sell the buyer. A telephone equipment company can make as much money changing telephone sockets and adding new ones as it made on selling the original switchboard.

Even if the profit on the initial sale is small, the annual profit may be many times more. So it may be worth losing all the initial profit (on price reductions, the cost of the presentation, and other selling expenses) to win the customer.

Lifetime Value reminds us not to ignore our loyal customers. It tells us not to despise the small orders they place, nor to economise on the cost of acquiring and keeping the customer.

HOW MANY CUSTOMERS BUY ROUTINELY FROM YOU?

How much of your personal purchasing is with a small number of suppliers? Table 50 shows typical personal and corporate purchases. Put a cross in the right place for each item.

You'll probably find that a lot of your purchasing is done with

How consistent is your shopping?		
•	**Few suppliers** *(You normally buy from 1–2 companies)*	**Many suppliers** *(You use many companies)*
Private purchasing *Newspapers* *Groceries* *Petrol* *Holiday* **Corporate purchasing** *(your firm)* *Car leasing* *Stationery* *Travel arrangements*		

Table 50 **Suppliers are dependent on loyal customers**

very few companies. It shows that fewer purchases are made by 'shopping around' than you might expect. That means that most suppliers rely on loyal customers who spend a lot of money with them. That probably applies to the products you sell.

Most of us prefer to buy from the same source continuously. It saves us from having to make yet one more decision in our already complex lives. If we change our supplier it's often unwillingly, and only because the first supplier has let us down in some way. *So you need to ensure that your customer is able to keep buying from you.*

The first step is to consider what your customers think of you. This is what we turn to next.

HOW ENTHUSIASTIC ARE CUSTOMERS ABOUT YOUR PRODUCT?

As Table 51 shows, the best customer is the **Advocate**, a customer who is so positive that he encourages others to buy your product.

Customer attitudes	
Advocate	Recommends your product to others. Acts like an unpaid salesman.
Positive	Is pleased with your product. Will be a referee if required.
Neutral	Is not involved with your product. Will re-order when necessary.
Disenchanted	Has experienced unsatisfactory performance from your company.
Hostile	Actively dissuades people from buying your product.

Table 51   **What proportion of your customers are in each category?**

At the other end of the scale is the **Hostile** buyer. This person discourages people from buying your product.

Do you know what proportion of *your* customers are in each category? And can you create a strategy for each of these groups? For example, the Advocate may need informal training and a supply of literature. The Hostile buyer will need urgent action – perhaps you can involve a senior manager?

These attitudes (from Advocate to Hostile) create buying behaviour. As can be seen in Table 52, customers' loyalty is similar to lovers'. It ranges from the Faithful to the Promiscuous, the Divorced and the Virgins.

You can set targets to move customers from their current band to the one above it. For example, what percentage of your occasional users could become regular users?

ARE YOUR CUSTOMERS SATISFIED?

Any company will tell you that customer satisfaction is important. But few know how important it really is. In Table 53, 73 per cent of customers were very satisfied with the product, and most

Purchase behaviour

Name	Level of purchase	Comment	Action
Faithful	Solus	These customers only buy from you	Consolidate your success. Add value to what you're currently offering
	Preferred	This group buys from you whenever it can	Anticipate change Offer exclusive benefits to these loyalists
Promiscuous	Regular users	Is there little loyalty in your market? How can you become a 'preferred' supplier?	Boost their loyalty by offering extra benefit or service
	Occasional users	Are you lower in the repertoire than your competitors? Do people prefer not to buy your products?	Undertake competitive benchmarking. Convert them to regular users
Divorced	Lapsed users	Why have they stopped buying? What will make them customers again?	Rectify faults. Make them an offer they can't refuse
Virgins	Non-users	Why aren't they buying?	Incentivise. Gain trial. Launch a different product which meets their needs

Table 52 **What percentage of buyers in your market fall into each of these categories?**

Customers satisfaction and subsequent re-purchase		
% of customers	who were	and of them, % which re-purchased
73	Very satisfied	86
24	Somewhat satisfied	49
3	Somewhat dissatisfied	11
0	Very dissatisfied	0
100		

Source: P-E International

Table 53 **How satisfaction affects re-purchase**

of them (86 per cent) repurchased. But of the 24 per cent who were 'somewhat satisfied', only a half (49 per cent) repurchased. For those who were 'somewhat dissatisfied', only 11 per cent repurchased.

Re-purchase falls off dramatically among customers who are less than very satisfied. In other words, only the best will do.

You can see signs of dissatisfaction in the insurance sales. Seventy per cent of insurance policies are cancelled within the first two years, according to AKG actuarial consultants. This results in huge losses for investors through surrender penalties. In the UK more than £1 billion worth of policies were surrendered in 1992. Eight out of ten insurance sales people leave their companies within two years of joining, and only eight in every 100 have been with their firm for four years. This points to over-selling and mis-selling. It also suggests that insurance sales people are failing to develop long-term relationships with their clients.

The same is true in love. If you don't satisfy your lover, you will find yourself abandoned. In the USA, 40 per cent of married women initiate divorce proceedings. A further 42 per cent create a double life for themselves, finding another primary relationship whether in work, with a lover or with children, while staying married. Thus 82 per cent leave their relationship in some form.

WARNING SIGNALS

A volcano gives warning that it is about to erupt. If you study your lover and customer, you'll be able to watch for signs of dissatisfaction. By checking for the symptoms shown in Table 54, you'll be able to see if they are becoming dissatisfied. If you spot these signs, you'll have to move fast to improve your quality of service. If you ignore them, you'll find your customer or lover abandons you for someone else.

Signs of dissatisfaction	
Your lover	**Your customer**
Moody, eyes cast down, won't look you straight in the eyes.	Reduces volume of orders
Won't do you small favours any more	Won't accept offers of lunch
Not in when you telephone	Spend less time in meetings with you
Has more social meetings	Meets representatives from other companies
Receives mysterious phone calls	Is evasive about the future
Complains more frequently	Complains more frequently

Table 54 **When you notice your customer behaving this way, you should take action to improve your service**

THE PROBLEM OF THE DISSATISFIED CUSTOMER

According to research carried out by TARP (Technical Assistance and Research Programmes) in the US, customers with bad experiences are twice as likely to tell others as those with good experiences. That means you could end up with a town full of people moaning about your service. So it is vital to provide good service and to make amends to those whom you fail.

Research also shows that customers who complain and whose problems are handled well are much more likely to carry on doing business than those whose complaints are ignored or poorly handled.

WELCOME COMPLAINTS

You should welcome complaints. A lover who complains is offering you the chance to change. A customer who complains is saying to you 'I want to continue buying from you, if you can resolve this problem'. It is the customer's way of saying, 'I still love you. I want to offer you another chance'.

Your customer may also be saying, 'Did you know you have this problem? If I'm suffering from this problem, so are many other customers. So I'm giving you advance notice. If you don't do something about it, it could affect a lot more people.'

According to one hairspray manufacturer, one in 2000 customers complain. They found this out through market research, asking purchasers, 'Have you been disappointed when you used this product? If so, what did you do about it?' Only one in 2000 people complained. Of the other 1999, less than half would be likely to re-purchase (as we have seen in Table 53).

According to US White House research, for every customer who complains there are 26 customers with problems and a further six with a serious problem. And in the US, people are more likely to complain about bad service. In Europe, people may not complain, but they are just as likely to stop using an unsatisfactory product or service.

COMPANIES ARE POOR AT SAYING SORRY

Not all complaints are handled well. Twenty-three per cent of complaints in the North East of England are rejected by rude and unhelpful staff, according to a survey by First Direct Bank. In the South West of the country, 22 per cent of complaints are simply ignored. Business has a lot of improvements to make in customer handling.

You can't get it right 100 per cent of the time. Sometimes you do thoughtless things that upset your customer or your lover. At times like this, only one word is strong enough – 'sorry'.

Customers need to hear the word 'sorry'. A *Daily Telegraph* journalist was delayed on a Virgin Airways flight, and had to take a £10 taxi fare to catch up. So he complained to Virgin. In reply he received a handwritten note from Richard Branson, starting with the words, 'sorry'. There was also a £10 cheque pinned to the note. What else could that journalist do but write an article in praise of Virgin?

Some service companies find it hard to be always right. An airline can be delayed by competitors' flights, by weather, and by traffic controllers. When that happens, an apology and an explanation can turn a customer from being Hostile to being an Advocate.

- **Don't be defensive**: Many companies respond defensively towards complainers. They react by justifying themselves. 'No one else has ever complained about that', said a Hoover engineer when a tumble drier mangled some tights the first time it was used.
- **Develop a mechanism to encourage complaints**: Encourage your customers to comment and complain at every opportunity. The more communication between customer and company, the more you're likely to keep the customer. Customer comments can be a useful source of new product ideas; a small unresolved complaint eventually becomes a giant sore. British Airways transatlantic sleeper service, and the hot food served on its London to Belfast route was initiated from customer feedback.
- **Resolve the complaint**: Now you've got customers actively

complaining, you'll have to resolve their complaints. A fast response is essential – nothing less than a reply by return of post is acceptable. Your holding letter should acknowledge the complaint and promise to investigate it. Your letter must look personal, even though the core of the letter is likely to be standardised. This means that the letter should be typed, never printed.

YOUR RELATIONSHIP IS UNDER ASSAULT

Other suitors are continually pursuing your lover. Everywhere, your lover sees sensual images and hears beckoning voices. If you don't maintain your relationship, your lover is likely to stray. The same is true of your customer. So it's worth considering *why* customers leave.

THE REASON WHY CUSTOMERS LEAVE

An important research finding was quoted at the 1992 National Communications Forum, Chicago. The study found that 68 per cent of customers who leave a supplier do so because of an attitude of indifference from one or more individuals in the supplier's organisation. In other words, they leave not for reasons of price or delivery, but because they think the supplier is indifferent to them.

In other words, *to keep a customer, you have to make him feel wanted*. What's more, reducing the number of customers lost by the company could increase profits by 25 per cent to 85 percent, depending on the product, according to Harvard Business Review.

A consultant accompanied me to one of my clients. After the meeting, he remarked what a relaxed and friendly group of people this company had. 'Unlike,' he went on, 'Many of the clients I meet, who are always moaning'. He didn't understand that the difference may have stemmed from the quality of the client servicing.

ACTION POINTS

♥ Look after existing customers. Generally, they are your best source of revenue.

♥ If measured over a long period, even the smallest customer's value is sizeable. So look after small customers as well as large ones.

♥ Relax about the cost of acquiring a new customer. Evaluate the payback over a sufficiently long period of time.

♥ Customers prefer to buy from their existing supplier. Often it is only poor product and service quality which drives them away.

♥ Assess whether your customers range from being Advocates to Hostile. Take appropriate action.

♥ Assess, too, the faithfulness of your customers. Take steps to improve their loyalty.

♥ Evaluate the satisfaction of your customers. Anything less than complete satisfaction will lead to desertions.

♥ Check for warning signs among your customers. Prompt action will be required.

♥ Welcome complaints. The complainer needs to be handled positively.

♥ Remember that your relationship is always under assault. Keep wooing your customers.

Seductive Service

You, the sales person, are the most important factor in determining customer perceptions of your business.

According to Table 55, 57 per cent of customers say the most important factor is the quality of their relationship with the primary contact in the supplier's organisation. It ranks even higher than product performance, the reputation of the company, or any other factor you could think of. In other words, it's *your* relationship, and *you* have to make it work.

Customer perceptions: the most important factors	
	%
Primary contact	57
Reputation of the company	29
Product performance	14
Total	100

Source: Learning International

Table 55 **You, the primary contact, are the most important factor in determining the customer's opinion of your company**

THE PROBLEMS YOU CAUSE

It's easy to think about the problems you cause your lover. They might include staying out late, drinking with friends, or failing to sympathise with your lover's problems.

But what about your customer? Some of the problems may be beyond your control, such as late deliveries or quality failures. But unless you exert pressure to rectify them, you'll lose the client.

And what about the failures for which you alone are responsible? Do you promise to provide information, and then forget

My lover	
The problems I cause	Solutions I can provide
1.	
2.	
3.	
4.	
5.	
My customer	
Problems I and my company cause	Solutions we can provide
1.	
2.	
3.	
4.	
5.	

Table 56 **Identifying and overcoming problems**

about it? Do you turn up late to appointments? Do you neglect to bring the right brochures with you?

Table 56 has space for you to identify the problems you cause your lover and your customer. Space is also provided for solutions.

AFTER SALES SERVICE

For some companies, half of all complaints arise from failure to read the instructions. This is sometimes because the instructions are too complicated to understand. So it is important to keep in contact with your customers, especially when they are new clients or if they have recently ordered a non-standard product or service.

If your product has to be installed, or the customer needs to be trained, it is in your interests to make it work properly. Even when the instructions are clearly explained and printed, people still get confused.

WHEN THE FIRST SALE WAS THE LAST

With increasing regulation over waste disposal, a local authority ordered a small incinerator for one of its schools. The incinerator was fired three times, each time emitting smoke and fumes. Eventually, the local authority sold it for little more than its scrap value.

The company lost any hope of winning any more contracts, despite the fact that the local authority planned to incinerate an increasing proportion of its waste over the next decade. Yet a small amount of help with that first installation could have led to many more orders.

TRAPS TO AVOID IN A MATURE RELATIONSHIP

Any body will grow slack if it isn't exercised. And any relationship can grow stale if you don't put effort into it. The same

Signs of inertia	
Inertia in love	**Inertia in selling**
You don't go out with your lover except for routine trips	You haven't changed your method of operating for a long time
You have stopped buying your lover presents except at Christmas and birthdays	You have stopped looking for new customers
You have stopped spending quality time together	Your list of customers hasn't changed
You have stopped saying, 'I love you'	You've stopped worrying about the service you deliver
You bicker; you fail to discuss problems properly	Your call rate has declined
You don't guard your lover's feelings	You have stopped making suggestions to your boss

Table 57 **Inertia sets in so gradually that you hardly notice**

applies to the relationship you have with your customer. Table 57 shows some of the signs of inertia setting in. If any of these factors apply to you, you need to start renewing your relationship.

HOW MUCH SERVICE CAN YOU PROVIDE?

As an individual the amount of love you can give your partner is limited by your other responsibilities. For example, the need to earn a living may restrict how often you go out together.

The amount of service your company can give a customer depends on how many customers it has. Take a can of baked beans. Its manufacturer may have ten major accounts, 1000 superstores, 25000 supermarkets, 2 million purchasers, and 8 million consumers. It can bestow huge amounts of affection on its ten *major accounts*. They will receive the same level of attention as a lover, with constant phone calls, personal visits and regular entertaining.

The next group – the *superstores* – also merit personal attention from senior sales staff. For the 25 000 *supermarkets*, the sales force will be expected to apply the same principles. This will include personal visits, little gifts and soothing words.

The marketing department will care for the *purchaser*, often the housewife, and the people she buys for, the *consumer*. Much of this love will be bestowed from a distance.

Advertising is the main way of demonstrating affection towards the consumer. Much advertising sets out to flatter or beguile the purchaser. It shows the ideal family eating Sunday lunch, or the fond mother getting her lovely children's clothes clean. Or it shows the responsible mother keeping the family's drains free from germs.

SEGMENTING CUSTOMERS BY WORTH

You can't lavish personal service on every customer. Some are too small to justify the investment. So you need to categorise customers by size of order.

At the top end will be a small number of high spending customers – your national accounts or **key accounts**. Many companies find that 80 per cent of their business comes from 20 per cent of their customers.

At the bottom will be a large number of small customers. As we saw in Lifetime Value, adding up all their business amounts to a sizeable income, so you can't afford to ignore these customers. You need a strategy to make them feel that you are looking after their needs.

In the middle will be a group of customers who provide solid revenue, probably year after year. You need to show them that you recognise their worth; and you need to express your affection to them.

The way to do all this is to categorise customers according to their worth, and provide an excellent, tailored level of service for each. Table 58 provides a structure for doing this.

Categorising customer service levels		
Category (*by annual order value*)	**Customer names**	**Target level of service**
1.		
2.		
3.		
4.		

Table 58   **What level of service should your customers receive? What level of service do they expect?**

ADOPTING SERVICE TO CUSTOMER PROFILE

Some customers will have distinct profiles. They may be co-operatives, or small businesses, or architects. We looked at segmenting your market in Chapter 2. Now you should decide how to provide a service which matches the needs of these segments. For example, they may require:

- different **frequency** of call (a visit per week, per fortnight, or a month);
- different **time** of call (some may need to be contacted after work hours);
- different **method** of call (telephone, personal visit);
- different information.

DO A QUALITY REVIEW

Your lover's view of your performance may be different from your own. You might walk around saying to yourself, 'I'm a sexy, successful person', while your lover may feel that you are inconsiderate and selfish. So it's important to find out your lover's perception. The same is true of your customer. Remember how we talked about the customer's attitude, from Advocate to Hostile? Through research you can find out how your customers feel about you. It is simply a case of asking the customer what he thinks of your product and service. Customers are usually flattered to be asked. They love giving their views. They see the fact finding mission as a sign of professionalism. They will also identify – with painful accuracy – areas where the work was less than perfect. You will make your customer feel important, and you will learn a surprising amount. The research should be carried out using a formal questionnaire, and the data from each questionnaire stored in a database, so that you can track trends over time.

The review should check how you perform on all the issues that are important to the client, such as price, delivery, quality and competence of personnel. On one recent job, we discovered that:

- our work was of a reasonably high standard;
- service was adequate but declined during the job (as the client thought it might);
- the project leader was difficult to get hold of.

This information was invaluable. It told us about the calibre of people we used, and it told us exactly where we could improve.

HONESTY IS THE BEST POLICY

Your lover has the right to expect integrity. That means monogamy, unless you have declared an open relationship.

Likewise, a customer has the right to expect the highest levels of integrity. This is particularly important where:

1. the product is sold to a sensitive market (for example to children); and
2. you receive a bonus for a sale.

A major manufacturer which has adopted an 'open book' policy with its suppliers says, 'We expect a supplier to be able to say to us: "Don't buy this particular product; it's rubbish" '.

Table 59 illustrates a code of conduct which sets the kind of standards required by customers today.

A code of conduct

Harm: You should not sell products which harm anyone or cause environmental damage. Potential dangers should be clearly marked.

Integrity: You should conform to the highest ethical standards. You should only sell products to customers who have a demonstrated need.

Competence: You should be competent in all tasks you undertake.

Conflict of interest: You should not have a financial interest which conflicts with the customer's needs. In the event of any conflict of interest, you should tell the customer in advance.

Confidentiality: You should not disclose any confidential information about a customer to anyone else, without first gaining the customer's approval.

Codes of practice: You should conform to the law and to relevant codes of practice appropriate to your business and profession.

Table 59 **Integrity is the basis of an honest relationship with the customer**

HOW TO STAY IN TOUCH

The best way to keep a customer is by staying in touch. Constant contact is an important element of good service. You may have to find reasons or pretexts for doing this. Some ways of achieving seductive service are shown in Table 60.

KEEP REWARDING YOUR LOVER

Do you reward your lover? Do you bring flowers? Do you say 'I love you'?

And do you do the same for your customer? It is good practice to reward the customer for his loyalty. Many companies agonise

---

Eleven ways to achieve seductive service

1. Phone the customer to see that the product has been delivered, and is working properly.
2. Arrange a review meeting a month after the product or service has been delivered to check the customer's satisfaction.
3. Send the customer clippings of magazine articles which might interest him.
4. Invite him to a sporting or cultural event.
5. Buy him lunch or drinks.
6. Find out the birthdays of his family members, and wish him well on those days. Include his wedding anniversary.
7. Give him your home phone number.
8. Tell him personally of any changes in prices or corporate policy.
9. Increase the frequency of visits.
10. Undertake a quality review.
11. Reward your customer through sales promotion (see below).

Table 60 **Maintaining contact with a customer**

about sales promotion. They fear that their promotions will go straight to existing customers who (they reckon) will buy anyway. But loyal customers keep your business going. Don't hesitate to reward them.

GOING OUT

Going out to an event is an important part of any relationship, whether with a lover or a buyer. As Table 61 suggests, outings can take many forms.

- **You can take your customer out.** Entertaining a customer will give you insights into his interests and his organisation. Similarly, joint selling activities could be a way of improving the relationship between a manufacturer and a key distributor.
- **You can even take your product out.** Display it at an exhibi-

Outings	
Your lover	**The buyer**
Disco, club	Lunch
Theatre	Sporting event
Film	Cultural event
Walk	Joint selling activities
Special interest club	

Table 61 **Getting out and about**

tion. Practice varies according to industry, from a major trade fair at Frankfurt, to a small display in a shopping mall. Events vary in the number of buyers who attend – and this can vary from year to year. The quality of attendance also varies – only you can make up your mind by comparing the cost of the exhibition against the orders won.

HOW MUCH FUN ARE YOU?

How much excitement, interest or fun do you give your customers? It's easy to become so locked into the effort of work that you seem grim to your customers. People in selling have to sing for their supper. Like a lover, they have to demonstrate that they are charming and entertaining.

The lover who each day comes home and talks only about his time at the office before slumping in front of the television is in danger of losing his spouse to someone more exciting.

Check your glamour factor. How interesting are you, compared with your competitors? What entertaining do you do? What do your offices look like? How are customers greeted?

DEVELOPING AN INDIVIDUAL RESPONSE

A customer must be given individual treatment. It is easy for us to imagine that we have a fixed range of products, and that our customers are all faceless 'buyers'.

Companies like things to be fixed, whether the product formula or the price. All production departments like to sell just one product, one which avoids short runs, colour changes and specially made products. But any company which wants to make life convenient for itself will soon be outsmarted by its competitors.

Treat every buyer as an individual. Consider his needs. Ask yourself, 'What would I want if I were him?' Push your company to be flexible in its response to customers' requirements. Table 62 provides space for you to write down the things that customise your product or service. Can you arrange delivery differently? Can you fit extras? Or can you cut out the frills?

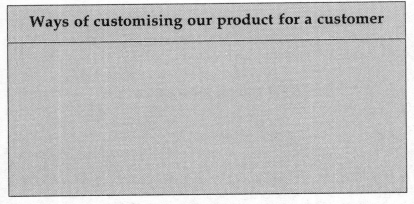

Ways of customising our product for a customer

Table 62 **Write down the various ways you could tailor your product and service to meet your customer's needs**

Extending your involvement over a customer

PHH is a fleet management business, which has developed a smart card that contains a car's service history. The card is linked to a diagnostic machine in garages so that drivers can see when items need replacing before they wear out. This type of preventative maintenance makes PHH an important part of the customer's fleet management team.

By extending its involvement with the customer, PHH becomes inextricably linked. This makes it difficult for the customer to use another supplier. Can you get this close to your customers?

THE SALES DEPARTMENT

It's easy for an office-based sales department to see themselves as just order-takers. *Nothing could be further from the truth.*

The first requirement is a screen-based information system, which enables staff to see the customer's ordering history. Then the sales person should remind the customer about:

1. new products.
2. special offers. A continuous programme of special offers will encourage customers to sample products which they might not otherwise try.
3. products for which his sales are down, year on year.

The sales person should develop a personal rapport with the customer (because customers are influenced by the friendliness of their suppliers). He should also collect and market information, for which the office-based sales department is the ideal channel.

WINNING SALES FROM TELEPHONE ENQUIRIES

Poorly handled sales enquiries can cost a company a fortune in lost sales. Incoming sales enquiries must be handled effectively. You should collect as much information about the enquirer as possible.

Take a consumer asking a lawnmower company for a brochure. The company could ask what size of garden he has. It could ask whether he prefers petrol or electrical mowers; where he prefers to shop, and how much he has to spend. This would allow the company to send not just a brochure but also recommend a choice of model, and perhaps supply a money-off voucher for that machine.

If the company has obtained the customer's telephone number, it could ring back to see what machine he actually bought, and whether he needed any help with it.

It is this level of service which will keep the customer loyal to that company. In three years' time, the company can mail the customer a leaflet showing the new models, and make a phone call to see whether he might upgrade his mower.

This example is taken from a consumer industry, but the same approach can be adopted for trade enquiries or industrial customers.

ACTION PONTS

♥ Remember that *you* are the main reason why the customer buys your product. That gives you a responsibility to get things right.

♥ Identify the problems that you and your business cause a customer, and seek to put them right.

♥ Catagorise your customers, and assess how much service you can give each group.

♥ Adapt your customer service to different customer profiles. Each group of customers may have a different sets of needs.

♥ Undertake a formal quality review with all main customers.

♥ Adopt a code of practice. Publicise it to your customers.

♥ Identify ways of staying in touch with your customers. Regular contact is a key factor in customer satisfaction.

♥ See how you can extend your links inside the customer's business.

♥ Check how customer enquiries are handled by your business, and how your sales department responds to customers. You could be losing a lot of business.

Summary

16

The Facts of Life

The theme of *Seductive Selling* is that love and selling are similar. Many similarities have been quoted throughout the book, and below is a summary of the main ones. Because the points are condensed, you may need to refer back to the text for a fuller explanation. The points act as a useful reminder of the book's main themes. Together, they sum up the philosophy of *Seductive Selling*.

Follow this philosophy and you'll be successful in selling and fortunate in love.

Chapter	The facts of life about your lover	The facts of life about your customer
1. *Sex and selling*	Love is a quest. You must find the person you desire, woo them, consummate the relationship, and then maintain it	You must find the buyer you need, build a rapport, gain a sale, and then maintain the relationship
	Being a good lover takes more than just wearing smart clothes	Selling takes more than just being a good conversationalist
2. *Who are you after?*	Ask yourself, 'Who would want me as a lover?'	Ask yourself, 'Who wants to buy my product?'

Chapter	The facts of life about your lover	The facts of life about your customer
	Ask yourself, 'Where would I find a lover?'	Ask yourself, 'Where would I find a customer?'
	You don't have to chase every potential lover: be selective	You don't want to pursue every potential customer: target your pursuit
	Go to the sort of places your potential lover is likely to visit	Go to the places where you will find a buyer. Don't overlook the less obvious places
	The more people of the opposite sex you meet, the greater your chances of finding love	The more customers you meet, the more you will sell
	Avoid lovers who carry sexual disease	Avoid financially unstable customers
	Take precautions by practising safe sex	Take precautions by credit checking, and by avoiding undue financial liability
3. *The customer*	Your lover wants a long-term relationship, not a one-night stand	The buyer wants a long term relationship, not one-off purchases
	Today partnerships are more equal. Lovers are more of a team	Today, selling is more complex. Customers have broader teams and expect greater involvement with the sales person

Chapter	The facts of life about your lover	The facts of life about your customer
4. *Your competitors*	Be aware who else is after your lover	Understand the competition. Do a benchmarking exercise. Work out how to beat the competitors
5. *Make the buyer warm to you*	You won't get love from someone who doesn't know you	A customer doesn't buy on a cold call
	You may meet a new lover through a mutual friend	Reach a customer by establishing a link
	A friend is more likely to make love if the atmosphere is right. Get your lover in the mood before asking for love	Get the customer in the right mood if you want to achieve a sale. A customer is more likely to buy when he initiates the enquiry, and when he needs to buy
	An informal or indirect approach may help you get a date	An indirect approach may help you get an appointment
6. *Getting through*	To get a date, you have to establish a rapport, assess that there is a willingness to talk further, and ask for the date	To get an interview, you have to establish a rapport, assess that there is a willingness to talk further, and ask for an appointment
7. *Seductive writing*	A love letter should be personal, focused on your lover, and fervent	Any communication with a customer should be personal, focused on the customer, and be honest

Chapter	The facts of life about your lover	The facts of life about your customer
8. The seduction process	People go on a date for two reasons: romance and sex	People attend a sales meeting for two reasons: to solve a problem and to sell their product
	If a man and woman can reconcile their different needs, they have a good relationship	If a buyer and seller can reconcile their different needs, the sale can go ahead
	Distinguish yourself from other people by the way that you care or the effort you put into the relationship	Differentiate a commodity product through customer service
	Lovers like gifts	Customers like samples
	Taking your lover out is part of the wooing process	Entertaining your customer should be part of the sales process
		You can also take your product out to exhibitions
	At the end of a date, make sure you stay in contact with your friend	After an exhibition, follow up the contacts you made
9. Building a relationship	To have an effective relationship, you need to be understanding, caring and responsive	To have an effective relationship, you need to be understanding, caring and responsive

Chapter	The facts of life about your lover	The facts of life about your customer
	Lovers play games. They can play hard to get	Customers play games. They can play hard to get
	By understanding your relationship with your lover, you can improve it	By understanding your relationship with your customer, you can improve it
10. *Use your body*	Body language tells a lover about his partner's readiness for love	Body language tells a seller about a customer's willingness to buy
	A lover's clothes are part of his image	Packaging is a brand's clothing. The seller's clothes and appearance are part of a company's image
11. *Seductive words*	Successful lovers encourage their lovers to talk about themselves	A successful sales person encourages the buyer to talk about himself
	Tell your lover, 'I love you'. Say it often and simply	Tell the customer you value his business
	Lovers want to be flattered	Compliment the customer
12. *Overcoming resistance*	Identify the reasons for a friend's resistance to making love, and decide how to overcome them	Identify the reasons for a customer's resistance to buying, and decide how to overcome them

Chapter	The facts of life about your lover	The facts of life about your customer
	The more a lover wants you, the more the lover will do for you	The more desirable a customer finds your product, the more he'll pay
13. *Closing in*	Go for it – ask for the date	Ask for the order
	You can get someone to sleep with you once, but the relationship is unlikely to flourish	You can trick the buyer into buying once, but the relationship will not flourish
	On a date, you can check to see if your partner is ready for love making	In selling, a trial close lets you see if the customer is ready to order
	Never use force against your lover	You can't force a customer to buy – more subtle techniques are needed.
	A trial marriage helps lovers decide whether they are compatible	Make it easy for your customer to buy by offering a low-effort, low-obligation trial
	Lovers need to feel wanted. They bestow their affection on those who care for them	Buyers need to feel wanted. They bestow their orders on those who care for them
	Your friend may want love as much as you	The buyer may need your services more than you imagine

Chapter	The facts of life about your lover	The facts of life about your customer
	If you lose a lover, find out why and change your approach next time	If you lose a sale, find out why, and change your approach next time
14. *Keeping it up*	Take care of your existing lover. Your existing lover will care for you	Look after your existing customer – he is more likely to give you more business
	Your lover probably does more for you than you realise	Over a lifetime of purchasing, your customer spends more than you might think
	A lover gives warning signals of dissatisfaction	A customer gives warning signals of his dissatisfaction
	If you can't give your lover satisfaction, your lover will look for someone who can	The customer needs customer satisfaction, or he'll start looking for another supplier
	A lover who complains is offering you a chance to change	A customer who complains wants to stay your customer, if you can change
	Saying sorry to your partner heals wounds	Saying sorry to a customer can make amends
	Your relationship is always under assault from other suitors	Your relationship is always under attack from competitors

Chapter	The facts of life about your lover	The facts of life about your customer
15. *Seductive service*	You cause your lover problems, which need to be resolved	You cause your partner problems, which need to be resolved
	A longstanding relationship with your lover can grow stale. You need to keep renewing it	A longstanding relationship with your customer can grow stale. You need to keep renewing it
	Your lover's view of you may be different from your own. Find out what your lover thinks	Your customer's view of you may be different from your own. Find out what he thinks
	Be honest with your lover	Develop a code of integrity for your customers
	Reward your lover with presents	Reward your customer through samples and sales promotion